LEISURE ARTS PRESENTS

THE SPIRIT OF CHRISTMAS

CREATIVE HOLIDAY IDEAS
BOOK FOUR

''When the fullness of time had come, God sent forth His Son, born of a woman ... ''

Foretold centuries before His coming, it is said that all creation rejoiced at the birth of the newborn King. And even now, nearly two thousand years later, the miracle of that first Christmas continues to touch our hearts. Each year through pageants, Nativities, and other celebrations, we reverently portray the events of that wondrous night, seeking to discover anew the wonderful gift of love. Though customs may vary, it is the desire to impart a bit of that same eternal love that is at the heart of all our holiday preparations. May this special book enrich your Christmas experience and help you spread the joy of the season to those you love!

LEISURE ARTS, INC.
Little Rock, Arkansas

THE SPIRIT OF CHRISTMAS

BOOK FOUR

EDITORIAL STAFF

Editor-in-Chief: Anne Van Wagner Young
Managing Editor: Sandra Graham Case
Creative Art Director: Gloria Hodgson
Assistant Editor: Susan Frantz Wiles
Production Directors: Jane Kenner Prather and
    Sherry Taylor O'Connor
Production Assistants: Kathy Rose Bradley,
    Diana Heien Suttle, and Ginger Ann Alumbaugh
Food Editor: Micah Land
Assistant Food Editor: Christy Kalder
Editorial Director: Dorothy Latimer Johnson
Editorial Assistants: Linda L. Trimble and
    Tammi Foress Williamson
Production Art Director: Melinda Stout
Production Artist: Linda Lovette
Art Production Assistants: Cindy Zimmerebner-Nassab,
    Kathleen Murphy, Diane M. Hugo, Susan Vandiver,
    Leslie Loring Krebs, Sondra Harrison Daniel, and
    Mike States
Photography Stylists: Karen Smart Hall, Jan Vinsant,
    and Judith Howington Merritt
Editorial Copy Assistants: Marjorie Lacy Bishop,
    Eva Marie Delfos, Darla Burdette Kelsay, and
    Tena Kelley Vaughn
Typesetters: Laura Glover Burris, Stephanie Cordero,
    and Vicky Fielder Evans

BUSINESS STAFF

Publisher: Steve Patterson
Controller: Tom Siebenmorgen
Retail Sales Director: Richard Tignor
Retail Marketing Director: Pam Stebbins
Retail Customer Services Director: Margaret Sweetin
Marketing Manager: Russ Barnett
Circulation Manager: Guy A. Crossley
Print Production Manager: Chris Schaefer

*''...and it was always said of him, that he knew
how to keep Christmas well, if any man alive
possessed the knowledge. May that be truly said of
us, and all of us!''*

— From *A Christmas Carol* by Charles Dickens

International Standard Book Number 0-942237-07-2

TABLE OF CONTENTS

TABLE OF CONTENTS
(Continued)

THE SHARING OF CHRISTMAS

Page 86

THE TASTES OF CHRISTMAS

Page 110

AMERICAN HERITAGE DINNER 112

HOLIDAY SWEETS 118

THE SIGHTS OF CHRISTMAS

Dressed up in holiday finery, our homes take on a special charm at Christmastime. Twinkling lights, cherished ornaments, and the fresh scent of evergreens blend to create a magical atmosphere. Laughter fills the air as we gather around a cozy fire to string popcorn and make our own special decorations. What a wealth of memories we create when trimming the tree becomes a family celebration! Warm in this circle of love, we share again the wonderful joys of Christmas.

*S*erene and quieting, a blanket of snow transforms the earth into a winter wonderland. Especially at Christmastime, this enchanting setting invites us to gather before a cozy fire and share the magic of the beautiful sight.

In this collection, the snow-kissed tree is home to a flock of tiny snowbirds. Woodsy pinecones, raffia-tied balls, pearly icicles, and handcrafted snowflakes enhance the delicate beauty. As a garland of snowballs winds about the tree, tiny lights twinkle like stars. Venturing forth on the snowy fleece skirting, a family of woodland bunnies brings a sense of awe to the scene.

A stately St. Nicholas graces the mantel, which is draped with a linen scarf embroidered with snowflakes. Glowing candles, boughs of evergreen, and pinecones nestled on doilies complement the arrangement. In the next room, a smaller tree shines with warmth, and simply wrapped gifts stand waiting to be opened.

This year, enjoy the peaceful white Christmas of your dreams. Instructions for the projects shown here and on the next three pages begin on page 13.

(*Opposite*) Echoing the ornaments on our **Winter Wonderland Tree** (*page 13*), graceful birds and fanciful snowflakes adorn this lace-trimmed **Snowbird Stocking** (*page 15*). The matching linen **Mantel Scarf** (*page 14*) is pictured on page 9.

This handsome **Winter White St. Nicholas** (*page 18*), crafted of crepe paper and cotton batting, is a replica of a Russian St. Nicholas from the early 1900's. In Russia, this noble Christmas gentleman is traditionally clad in ermine robes, so we textured the trim on his coat to resemble this regal fur.

Penning holiday greetings will be a pleasure with these elegant **Embossed Christmas Cards** (*page 15*). With every card you write, you can send your own gentle wishes for a magical white Christmas.

The **Winter Wonderland Tree** *(page 13)* is a snow-covered dream, made even lovelier with subtle earth-tone trimmings. Little birds nestle among its branches, which are encircled by a glistening **Snowball Garland** *(page 19)*. Lustrous strands of pearls complement woodsy **Bleached Pinecones** *(page 19)* and **Papier Mâché Ornaments** *(page 19)*. **Scherenschnitte Snowflakes** *(page 13)* and **Bargello Snowflakes** *(page 13)* drift softly through the boughs, while star-shaped lights illuminate this vision in white.

WINTER WONDERLAND TREE
(Shown on page 8)

The quiet elegance of a winter forest scene is brought indoors to decorate this Winter Wonderland tree. Snowy white and shades of woodland brown gleam on a background of dark greenery. This 6½ foot flocked tree sprinkled with iridescent glitter takes on extra sparkle when strands of purchased white star lights are strung among its branches.

Fashioned from plastic foam balls and dusted with iridescent snow, a garland of snowballs winds gracefully around the tree. Three-dimensional snowflakes cut from craft paper are perfect companions for the two sizes of snowflakes stitched on needlepoint canvas. Covered with brown paper and topped with raffia, glass ball ornaments continue the theme of natural colors. Pinecones bleached to a golden tan are also easy to make. Instructions for these projects are included in the following pages.

Gleaming pearly icicles are made by cutting pearl garland into 7" lengths and hanging the lengths from branches with nylon line. Touched with blushes of peach, dozens of purchased white snowbirds complete the tree ornaments.

The tree is crowned with a spray of purchased white twigs, and yards of fleece batting cover the base to form a soft blanket of snow. The snowy ground accents the purchased papier mâché bunnies that have gathered around to admire the Winter Wonderland Tree.

BARGELLO SNOWFLAKES (Shown on page 12)

For each snowflake, you will need 14 mesh brown bargello canvas (4" square for each large snowflake or 3" square for each small snowflake), Ecru Paternayan Persian yarn (color #261), masking tape, and a #22 tapestry needle.

1. (**Note:** If making several snowflakes, leave at least 1" between snowflakes and stitch snowflakes on one large piece of canvas.) Cover edges of canvas with masking tape. Using 2 strands of yarn and Gobelin Stitch, page 157, follow chart and stitch desired snowflake on canvas.
2. Following grey cutting lines on chart, cut out snowflake.
3. For hanger, thread one 10" strand of yarn through stitches at top back of snowflake; knot ends of yarn together.

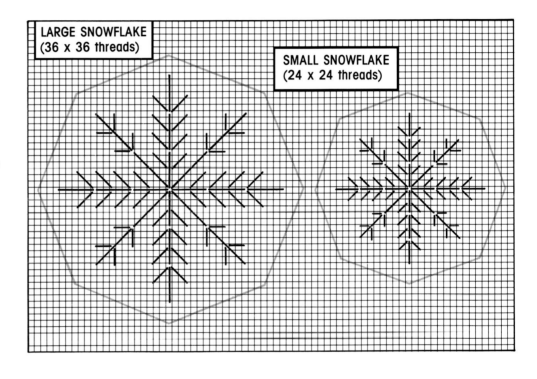

LARGE SNOWFLAKE (36 x 36 threads)

SMALL SNOWFLAKE (24 x 24 threads)

SCHERENSCHNITTE SNOWFLAKES (Shown on page 12)

For each snowflake, you will need two 6" squares of brown craft paper; thread to match paper; small, sharp-pointed scissors; graphite transfer paper; removable tape; and tracing paper.

1. Trace snowflake pattern onto tracing paper.
2. Fold one piece of craft paper in half. Matching dashed line on pattern to fold on craft paper, use transfer paper to transfer pattern. Repeat for remaining piece of craft paper.
3. To cut out each snowflake, use tape to hold edges of paper together. Beginning with smaller areas, cut out each snowflake.

4. Unfold snowflakes and place together, matching fold lines. Machine stitch on fold line, leaving 5" of thread at one end (top).
5. For hanger, knot ends of thread together.
6. Refer to photo to fold snowflakes away from stitching line.

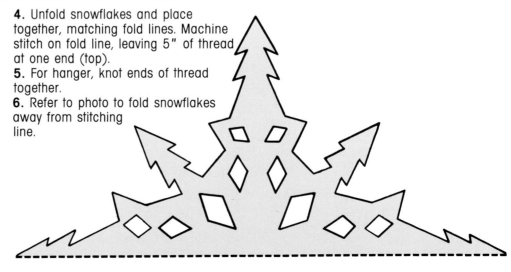

13

MANTEL SCARF (Shown on page 9)

You will need two pieces of light beige medium-weight linen fabric (see Step 1 for amount), white embroidery floss, ½"w white lace trim, thread to match fabric, glue stick, hot-iron transfer pencil, tracing paper, embroidery hoop, and blocking board and T-pins (optional).

1. For scarf measurements, measure length of mantel and add 5"; measure width of mantel and add 6". Cut two pieces of linen the determined measurements. Set one piece of linen aside for backing.
2. To mark side seams, machine baste across remaining piece of linen 2½" from one short edge; repeat for remaining short edge.
3. Glue pieces of tracing paper together to form a strip equal to length of mantel. Beginning at center and working toward the ends of the strip, trace scarf pattern onto tracing paper strip, repeating as many times as necessary along length of paper.
4. Turn tracing paper strip over and draw over lines of design with transfer pencil. With transfer pencil side down, center traced strip on marked piece of linen with bottoms of scallops 2" from one long edge of linen; pin in place. Following manufacturer's instructions, transfer design onto fabric.
5. Machine baste along transferred scalloped line.
6. (**Note: Embroidery Stitch Diagrams** are shown on page 158. Use 4 strands of floss unless otherwise stated.) Following Stitch Key and working French Knots close together along dotted lines, stitch design.
7. To block stitched piece and remove transfer lines, follow **Blocking Stitched Pieces**, page 156, or have an experienced dry cleaner clean and block the stitched piece.
8. Trim stitched piece ½" from machine-basted lines. Use stitched piece as a pattern and cut out backing.
9. With right sides together and leaving an opening for turning, use a ½" seam allowance and sew pieces together. Trim seam allowances to ⅛"; clip curves and cut corners diagonally. Turn right side out; press. Sew final closure by hand.
10. Whipstitch lace trim to scalloped edge of mantel scarf.

Stitch Key
1 — Backstitch
2 — Satin Stitch
3A — French Knot (4 strands)
3B — French Knot (6 strands)

MANTEL SCARF

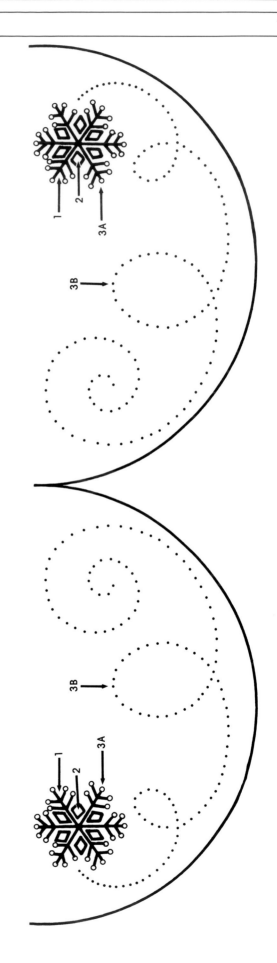

EMBOSSED CHRISTMAS CARDS (Shown on page 11)

You will need 6¼" x 9" sheets of stationery with matching envelopes, permanent felt-tip pen with fine point, one 8½" x 11" sheet of acetate, cutting mat or thick layer of newspapers, craft knife, removable tape, and plastic burnisher with pointed tip (available at art supply stores) or small plastic crochet hook.

1. Use pen to trace desired designs onto acetate. For snowflake, trace half of snowflake, then reposition acetate to trace remaining half of snowflake.
2. Place acetate on cutting mat and use craft knife to cut out designs.
3. For each card, match short edges and fold one sheet of stationery in half. Refer to photo to position stencil on front of card; using removable tape, tape stencil in place.
4. Turn card over and place stencil side down on a smooth, hard surface; unfold card.
5. Using side of burnisher tip or rounded end of crochet hook, gently rub over each design to produce outline. To emphasize design, use point of burnisher or large end of crochet hook to trace over outline of design. Remove stencil.
6. For each envelope, refer to photo to position stencil on right side of envelope flap and tape in place. Follow Steps 4 and 5 to emboss design on envelope flap.

SNOWBIRD STOCKING (Shown on page 10)

You will need two 16" x 22" pieces of light beige medium-weight linen fabric, two 14" x 20" pieces of fabric for lining, 15 skeins of white embroidery floss, 1¼ yds of ½"w white lace trim, 1⅔ yds of ⅛"w white satin ribbon, thread to match fabrics, tracing paper, hot-iron transfer pencil, embroidery hoop, and blocking board and T-pins (optional).

1. Matching arrows to form one pattern, trace stocking pattern, pages 16 and 17, onto tracing paper.
2. Turn pattern over and draw over lines of stocking and design with transfer pencil. With transfer pencil side down, position traced pattern on one piece of linen; pin in place. Following manufacturer's instructions, transfer design onto fabric.

3. Machine baste along transferred outline of stocking.
4. (**Note: Embroidery Stitch Diagrams** are shown on page 158. Use 4 strands of floss unless otherwise stated.) Following Stitch Key, page 16, and working French Knots close together along dotted lines, stitch design.
5. To block stitched piece and remove transfer lines, follow **Blocking Stitched Pieces**, page 156, or have an experienced dry cleaner clean and block the stitched piece.
6. Trim stitched piece ½" from machine-basted line. Use stitched piece as a pattern and cut one backing and two lining pieces from fabrics.
7. (**Note:** Use a ½" seam allowance.) For stocking, place stitched piece and backing piece right sides together. Leaving top edge open, sew pieces

together. Clip curves and turn right side out; press. Press top edge ½" to wrong side.
8. For lining, place lining pieces right sides together. Leaving top edge open, sew pieces together. Press top edge ¾" to wrong side. With wrong sides together, insert lining into stocking.
9. For hanger, cut one 5" length of ribbon. Matching ends, fold ribbon in half. Pin ends of ribbon between lining and stocking at right seamline.
10. Slipstitch lining to stocking and, at the same time, securely sew hanger in place.
11. Referring to photo, make a multi-loop bow from remaining ribbon; tack bow to stocking.
12. Referring to photo, whipstitch lace trim to edge of stocking.

Stitch Key
1 — Padded Satin Stitch
2 — Satin Stitch
3A — French Knot (4 strands)
3B — French Knot (6 strands)
4 — Buttonhole Stitch
5 — Backstitch

WINTER WHITE ST. NICHOLAS (Shown on page 11)

You will need one 12"h plastic foam cone, one 2" long plastic foam egg, Sculpey modeling compound, craft stick, acrylic paint (see Step 4 for colors), small round paintbrush, #0 liner paintbrush, matte clear acrylic spray, small amount of polyester fiberfill, 100% cotton batting, white crepe paper, masking tape, one 15" length of 18-gauge wire, needle nose pliers, white thread, craft glue, size 14 steel crochet hook, hot glue gun, glue sticks, and Design Master® glossy wood tone spray (available at craft stores).

1. For head, cover egg with a ⅜" thick layer of modeling compound. For beard, refer to **Figs. 1a** and **1b** and add more modeling compound to one side of small end of egg.

Fig. 1a

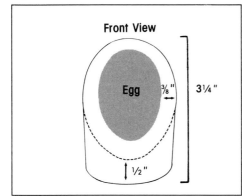

Front View

Egg   ⅜"   3¼"

½"

Fig. 1b

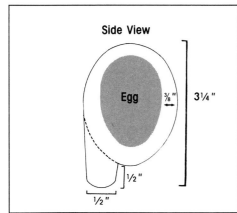

Side View

Egg   ⅜"   3¼"

½"

½"

2. For face, refer to **Fig. 2a** and use edge of craft stick to press approximately ¼" deep lines into modeling compound. Referring to photo and **Fig. 2b**, use stick to round areas between lines for brow, nose, cheeks, and mustache. Features should be more pronounced and deeper than they appear in photo.

Fig. 2a

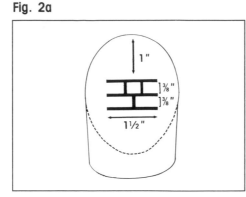

1"

1½"   ⅜"
⅜"

Fig. 2b

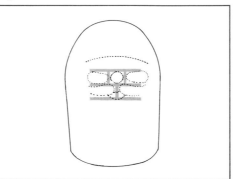

3. Gently press head into position on top of cone. Remove head from cone and follow manufacturer's instructions to harden modeling compound. Allow to cool. Applying glue to bottom of head only, hot glue head to top of cone.
4. Referring to photo and **Fig. 3**, paint head as follows:

- face — lt pink
- cheeks and nose — pink
- mouth — red
- eyes — black
- highlights in eyes — white
- eyebrows, mustache, and beard — white

Allow paint to dry. Spray head with two coats of acrylic spray, allowing to dry between coats.

Fig. 3

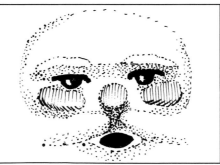

5. Cut ten 4" x 18" strips of batting. To fill out body, begin just below beard and wrap layers of strips around remainder of cone.
6. For arms, cut one 15" x 20" piece of batting. Referring to **Fig. 4**, cut one 1½" x 10" strip from each side of batting; discard strips. Use pliers to bend each end of wire ¼" to one side. Use masking tape to tape wire at center of uncut end of batting (**Fig. 4**). Roll batting snugly around wire.

Fig. 4

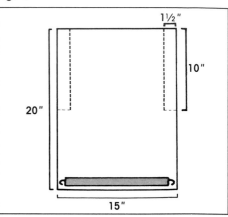

1½"

10"

20"

15"

7. (**Note:** When covering batting rolls with paper, cut and wrap paper so that grain runs along length of roll.) Cut one 20" x 10" piece of crepe paper. Center arm batting roll along one long edge of paper and roll paper around batting. Use craft glue to secure.
8. To form one hand, twist paper slightly at one end of arm batting roll. Tie thread tightly around paper at twist. Referring to **Fig. 5a**, turn paper wrong side out over end of batting. Referring to **Fig. 5b**, tie thread around paper to form wrist. Trim excess thread. Put a drop of craft glue into opening at end of hand and glue opening closed. Repeat to form remaining hand.

Fig. 5a   **Fig. 5b**

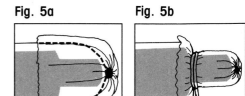

9. Center arms at top of cone behind and below head, with seam side of arms at back. Bend each arm down 1" from side of cone to form shoulders. Bend arms into desired position. Remove arms from cone.

WINTER WHITE ST. NICHOLAS (continued)

10. For coat, cut one 30" x 12" piece each from batting and crepe paper. With one long edge even with bottom of cone, wrap batting around body; wrap paper around body. Use craft glue to secure paper at center front of body.

11. For arm openings in coat, refer to **Fig. 6** and cut notches in paper and batting. Fold top edges of coat down even with bottoms of notches. Hot glue arms to cone and base of head. Fold top edges of coat back up; tuck top of coat under beard in front. Use craft glue to glue top edges of coat to arms in front and back.

Fig. 6

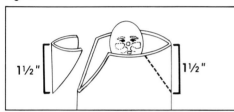

12. For trim on each sleeve, cut one 5" square of batting and one 7" square of crepe paper. Fold one edge of batting ½" to one side; continue folding to make a flattened roll. Center roll along one edge of paper and roll paper around batting; use craft glue to secure.

13. For bottom coat trim, cut one 18" x 10" piece of batting and one 20" x 8" piece of crepe paper. Fold one long edge of batting ¾" to one side; continue folding to make a flattened roll. Center roll along one long edge of paper and roll paper around batting; use craft glue to secure.

14. For front coat trim, cut one 22" x 13" piece of batting and one 26" x 8" piece of crepe paper (pieced as necessary). Fold one long edge of batting 1" to one side and repeat Step 13 to complete trim.

15. For hat trim, cut one 8" x 10" piece of batting and one 10" x 6" piece of crepe paper. Fold one short edge of batting ¼" to one side and repeat Step 13 to complete trim.

16. For ermine look on trim pieces, punch crochet hook through paper and pull a small amount of batting through layers of paper; refer to photo and repeat at desired intervals. Be careful not to tear paper when pulling batting through.

17. (**Note:** Use craft glue to glue trims in place.) Refer to photo and glue sleeve trim around each wrist, overlapping ends of trim at back of arm. Glue bottom coat trim around bottom of coat, overlapping ends at center front of coat. Glue front coat trim around neck and down front of coat; glue end of trim to bottom of cone under front edge of coat.

18. For hat, cut one 3" dia. circle of crepe paper. Refer to photo to position hat trim around head, overlapping ends at back of head. Remove trim from head and glue overlapping ends together. Place cotton ball-sized piece of fiberfill on top of head. Center paper circle over fiberfill and glue edges of circle to head. Press ring of trim onto head over paper; use craft glue to secure.

19. Spray St. Nicholas **very lightly** with wood tone spray.

SNOWBALL GARLAND (Shown on page 12)

You will need 1½", 2", 2½", and 3" dia. plastic foam balls; foam brush; craft glue; iridescent artificial snow; heavy thread (buttonhole twist); waxed paper; two small buttons; and 18" of 18-gauge florist wire.

1. Press foam balls with hands to form irregularly shaped "snowballs".
2. Pour snow into a medium bowl. Use foam brush to apply an even coat of glue to each ball. Roll each ball in snow and place on waxed paper; allow to dry.
3. For garland, cut desired length of thread and tie one button to one end.

Form wire as shown in **Fig. 1** and tie remaining end of thread to wire loop. Insert straight end of wire through one snowball and pull thread through. Continue stringing snowballs on thread until snowballs are approximately 6" from wire loop; cut thread. To secure remaining end of garland, tie remaining button to end of thread.

Fig. 1

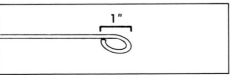

BLEACHED PINECONES
(Shown on page 12)

You will need pinecones, household liquid bleach, large bucket, clear glass plate or glass bacon press, a rock to weight plate, and foil-lined baking sheet.

Note: For best results, do this project outdoors on a sunny day. Bleach should only be used in a well-ventilated area. Caution should be taken not to splash bleach on clothing.

1. Place pinecones in bucket; add bleach to cover pinecones. Place plate or bacon press on pinecones and weight with rock to keep pinecones submerged in bleach. Allow to sit for five hours. Pinecones will close.
2. Remove pinecones from bleach. Place pinecones on baking sheet in oven at 250 degrees for several hours until pinecones open completely. Drying time will vary according to size of pinecones.

PAPIER MÂCHÉ ORNAMENTS
(Shown on page 12)

For each ornament, you will need one 2" dia. glass ball ornament, craft glue, brown craft paper, raffia, craft knife, hot glue gun, and glue sticks.

1. Cut paper into approximately forty ¼" x 7¼" strips. In a small bowl, mix one part craft glue to one part water. Dip one strip in glue and pull between fingers to remove excess glue. Place one short edge of strip at top of metal cap and wrap strip around ball, smoothing wrinkles with fingers. Alternating sides, repeat with remaining strips until ball is covered; allow to dry.
2. Use craft knife to trim excess paper even with top of metal cap.
3. Tie several strands of raffia into an approximately 4" wide bow with streamers. Referring to photo, hot glue bow to one side of ornament.

A WEE MERRY CHRISTMAS

Tales of wee people who come out while we're asleep have enchanted children around the world for centuries. In Scandinavian countries, families have passed down stories of the Julnisse (meaning "Christmas gnome"), who is said to bring good fortune to the household if he is treated well. To ensure his favor, the children leave a bowl of rice pudding or porridge for the gnome each Christmas Eve. This tiny fellow is seldom seen (except by animals or perhaps the children), but it is said that he wears a pointed red cap and long red stockings.

In this collection, stuffed "gingerbread" gnomes of painted muslin peek out from the tree and stand shyly about the room. Because gnomes sleep during the day and come out to work and play at night, beeswax moons and stars hang among the branches to light their way. A garland of red wooden beads traces their path about the tree. Giant stockings march across a mantel arranged with a woodland scene, and gnome-shaped cookies adorn a tiny tree.

Instructions for the projects shown here and on the next four pages begin on page 26. This year, invite a family of gnomes into your home for an enchanting Christmas!

Because woodcutting is a traditional task for gnomes, a stack of firewood makes an appropriate station for a greeting committee of **Gnomes** *(page 26)*.

Stitched with an attractive vine of leaves and hearts, this **Redwork Table Runner** *(page 31)* makes a lovely accessory that you'll want to use all year.

Trusted and loved by animals, **Gnomes** *(page 26)* move freely about farm and forest. To provide a woodland setting for a gnome to visit with fleecy **Sheep** *(page 29)* and other creatures, boughs of evergreen and sprays of nandina berries can be arranged on a mantel or tabletop.

With its simple red-on-white embroidered pattern, this **Redwork Welcome Pillow** *(page 30)* will greet your guests with Old World charm.

Reminiscent of the long red stockings worn by gnomes, these roomy knitted **Stockings** *(page 28)* are perfect for holding lots of Christmas goodies.

With a star-shaped **Beeswax Ornament** *(page 29)* overhead and a light dusting of snow on the evergreens and nandina berries, these **Gnomes** *(page 26)* are out for a Christmas Eve stroll. Nestled in an antique sifter, the arrangement makes an enchanting decoration for the wall or door.

(Opposite) Festive red icing brightens spicy gingerbread cookies on the **Cookie Tree** *(page 26)*. Patterned after antique German Nativity figures, a flock of woolly **Sheep** *(page 29)* gathers at its base to call on their wee friends.

COOKIE TREE
(Shown on page 24)

You will need Gingerbread dough (recipe follows), paring knife, tracing paper, 18"h feather tree, purchased tubes of red decorator frosting, and needle and nylon line (for hangers).

1. Trace cookie gnome and heart patterns onto tracing paper and cut out.
2. Place patterns on dough and use knife to cut around patterns. Bake as directed in recipe.
3. Referring to photo, frost cookies. Allow frosting to harden at room temperature for several hours.
4. For each hanger, use needle to thread 4" of nylon line through top of each cookie. Knot ends of line together.
5. Hang cookies on tree.

GINGERBREAD
- ¼ cup butter or margarine, softened
- 3 tablespoons firmly packed brown sugar
- 2 tablespoons granulated sugar
- 3 tablespoons maple syrup
- 1½ tablespoons molasses
- 1 egg
- 2 cups all-purpose flour
- 1 teaspoon baking soda
- ¼ teaspoon salt
- ¼ teaspoon ground allspice
- ¼ teaspoon ground cinnamon
- ¼ teaspoon ground cloves
- ¼ teaspoon ground ginger

In a medium mixing bowl, cream butter and sugars. Blend in maple syrup, molasses, and egg.

In another bowl, combine flour, baking soda, salt, and spices. Stir into creamed mixture. Wrap dough in plastic wrap and refrigerate at least 2 hours.

Preheat oven to 350 degrees. On a lightly floured surface, use a floured rolling pin to roll out dough to ⅛-inch thickness. Cut out cookies as indicated in instructions. Transfer cookies to lightly greased baking sheets. Bake 8 to 10 minutes or until lightly browned. Remove cookies from pans and cool on wire racks.
Yield: about 3 dozen 2½-inch cookies

GNOMES (Shown on page 22)

For each small gnome, you will need two 8" x 12" pieces of muslin fabric and 8" of nylon line for hanger (optional).
For each large gnome, you will need two 12" x 19" pieces of muslin fabric and transparent tape.
You will also need gesso, red and brown acrylic paint, matte water-based varnish, thread to match fabric, polyester fiberfill, small crochet hook (to turn fabric), foam brushes, tracing paper, and fabric marking pencil.

1. For small gnome pattern, follow **Transferring Patterns**, page 156. For large gnome pattern, use head and body patterns, page 27, and follow **Transferring Patterns**, page 156; matching arrows to form one pattern, tape patterns together.
2. Use desired pattern and fabric pieces and follow **Sewing Shapes**, page 156. Firmly stuff gnome with fiberfill; sew final closure by hand.
3. Apply two coats of gesso to gnome, allowing to dry between coats.
4. Referring to photo, paint gnome; allow to dry.
5. Apply one coat of varnish to gnome; allow to dry.
6. If hanger is desired for small gnome, thread nylon line through top of hat; knot ends of line together.

SMALL GNOME

COOKIE GNOME

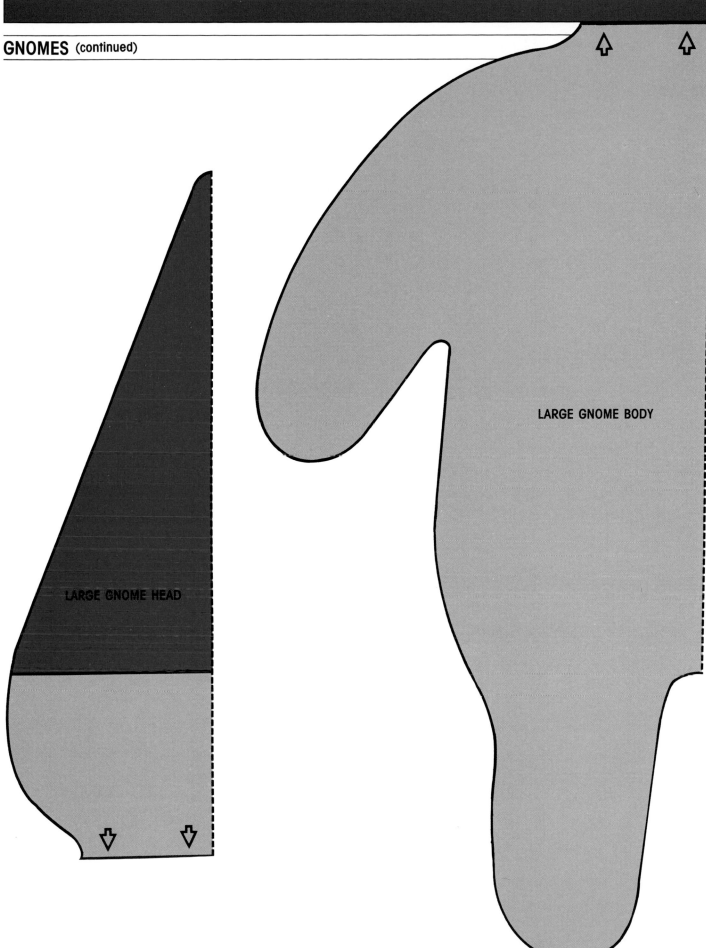

LARGE GNOME HEAD

LARGE GNOME BODY

STOCKINGS (Shown on pages 20, 21, and 25)

ABBREVIATIONS

CC	Contrasting Color
K	knit
MC	Main Color
P	purl
PSSO	pass slipped stitch over
st(s)	stitch(es)
tog	together

★ — work instructions following ★ as many **more** times as indicated in addition to the first time.

( ) — contains explanatory remarks

MATERIALS

For Narrow-striped Stocking, you will need Worsted Weight Yarn, approximately:
    MC (White) — 2 ounces (58 grams, 126 yards)
    CC (Red) — 3 ounces (86 grams, 189 yards)
For Broad-striped Stocking, you will need Worsted Weight Yarn, approximately:
    MC (White) — 2 ounces (58 grams, 126 yards)
    CC (Red) — 3 ounces (86 grams, 189 yards)
For Solid Stocking, you will need Worsted Weight Yarn, approximately:
    MC — 3½ ounces (100 grams, 220 yards)
    CC — 1½ ounces (43 grams, 94 yards)
Straight knitting needles, sizes 7 (4.50 mm) **and** 9 (5.50 mm) **or** sizes needed for gauge
3 Stitch holders
Markers
Yarn needle

GAUGE: With smaller size needles, in Stockinette Stitch, 20 sts and 26 rows = 4"
DO NOT HESITATE TO CHANGE NEEDLE SIZE TO OBTAIN CORRECT GAUGE.

INSTRUCTIONS

CUFF

With larger size needles and CC, cast on 50 sts **loosely**.
Work in K1, P1 ribbing for 4": 50 sts.

LEG

Change to smaller size needles.

Narrow-striped Stocking

Row 1 (Right side): With CC knit across.
Row 2: Purl across.
Row 3: With MC knit across.
Row 4: Purl across.
Rows 5-120: Repeat Rows 1-4, 29 times.

Broad-striped Stocking

Row 1 (Right side): With MC knit across.
Row 2: Purl across.
Row 3: Knit across.
Row 4: Purl across.
Rows 5-8: With CC work in Stockinette Stitch (knit 1 row, purl 1 row) for 4 rows.
Rows 9-120: Repeat Rows 1-8, 14 times.

Solid Stocking

Row 1 (Right side): With MC knit across.
Row 2: Purl across.
Rows 3-120: Work in Stockinette Stitch (knit 1 row, purl 1 row).

LEFT HEEL

Note: When instructed to slip a stitch, always slip as if to **purl**, unless otherwise specified.
Row 1: Slip 16 sts onto a st holder (Right Heel), slip 18 sts onto a second st holder (Top of Foot), with CC slip 1, knit across: 16 sts.
Row 2: Purl across.
Row 3: Slip 1, knit across.
Rows 4-15: Repeat Rows 2 and 3, 6 times.
Short Rows (to form corner of Heel): P2, P2 tog, P1, turn; slip 1, K3, turn; P3, P2 tog, P1, turn; slip 1, K4, turn; P4, P2 tog, P1, turn; slip 1, K5, turn; P5, P2 tog, P1, turn; slip 1, K6, turn; P6, P2 tog, P1, turn; slip 1, K7, turn; P7, P2 tog, P1, turn; slip 1, K8, turn; P8, P2 tog: 9 sts.
Slip remaining sts onto st holder.

RIGHT HEEL

With **right** side facing, slip sts from Right Heel st holder onto needle.
Row 1: With CC knit across.
Row 2: Slip 1, purl across.
Rows 3-14: Repeat Rows 1 and 2, 6 times.
Short Rows: K2, slip 1 as if to **knit**, K1, PSSO, K1, turn; slip 1, P3, turn; K3, slip 1 as if to **knit**, K1, PSSO, K1, turn; slip 1, P4, turn; K4, slip 1 as if to **knit**, K1, PSSO, K1, turn; slip 1, P5, turn; K5, slip 1 as if to **knit**, K1, PSSO, K1, turn; slip 1, P6, turn; K6, slip 1 as if to **knit**, K1, PSSO, K1, turn; slip 1, P7, turn; K7, slip 1 as if to **knit**, K1, PSSO, K1, turn; slip 1, P8, turn; K8, slip 1 as if to **knit**, K1, PSSO: 9 sts.

GUSSET AND INSTEP SHAPING

Note: Continue with color pattern established in leg.
Row 1: With color used in Row 1 of established leg pattern, pick up 7 sts on inside of Right Heel, knit 18 sts from st holder, pick up 7 sts on inside edge of Left Heel, knit 9 sts from Left Heel st holder: 50 sts.
Row 2 and all WRONG side rows: Purl across.
Row 3: K 14, K2 tog, K 18, slip 1 as if to **knit**, K1, PSSO, K 14: 48 sts.
Row 5: K 13, K2 tog, K 18, slip 1 as if to **knit**, K1, PSSO, K 13: 46 sts.
Row 7: K 12, K2 tog, K 18, slip 1 as if to **knit**, K1, PSSO, K 12: 44 sts.
Row 9: K 11, K2 tog, K 18, slip 1 as if to **knit**, K1, PSSO, K 11: 42 sts.
Row 11: K 10, K2 tog, K 18, slip 1 as if to **knit**, K1, PSSO, K 10: 40 sts.
Rows 13-32: Work in Stockinette Stitch in established color pattern.

TOE SHAPING

Row 1: With CC K7, K2 tog, K1, place marker, K1, slip 1 as if to **knit**, K1, PSSO, K 14, K2 tog, K1, place marker, K1, slip 1 as if to **knit**, K1, PSSO, K7: 36 sts.
Row 2: Purl across.
Row 3: ★ Knit to within 3 sts of marker, K2 tog, K1, slip marker, K1, slip 1 as if to **knit**, K1, PSSO; repeat from ★ once **more**, knit across: 32 sts.
Row 4: Purl across.
Rows 5-10: Repeat Rows 3 and 4, 3 times: 20 sts.
Bind off all sts.

FINISHING

With **right** sides together and beginning at Toe, sew seam to within 2" of top edge; with **wrong** sides together, sew remaining seam. Fold Cuff over.
For hanging loop, braid three 6" lengths of yarn together. Fold braided length in half to form a loop. Stitch ends of loop to seam at top of Cuff.

SHEEP (Shown on page 24)

For each sheep, you will need Sculpey modeling compound; one 4" x 6" piece of artificial lamb fleece; four 2¼" kitchen matches; craft knife; craft glue; red, white, and black acrylic paint; small round paintbrush; #00 liner paintbrush; 4" of ⅛"w red satin ribbon; ⅛" dia. jingle bell; and craft stick (optional).

1. Knead modeling compound to make it pliable.
2. (**Note:** For Steps 2 – 6, use fingers or craft stick to smooth surface of modeling compound.) For body, form a 1" x 2¼" x 1" block of modeling compound.
3. For neck, form a ½" block of modeling compound. Center neck on top at one end of body and smooth seam to bond (**Fig. 1**).

Fig. 1

4. For head, form an approximately ⅜" thick piece of modeling compound into a 1¼" wedge-shaped piece. For ears, pull out two corners of wedge ⅜" and pinch slightly (**Fig. 2**).

Fig. 2

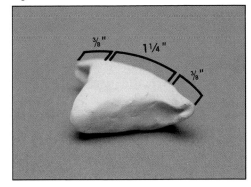

5. Referring to **Fig. 3**, attach head to neck, smoothing seam to bond.

Fig. 3

6. For legs, use craft knife to cut colored tips from matches. Insert ¾" of each matchstick into underside of body. Shape compound around matchsticks to form tops of legs (**Fig. 4**). Adjust legs to prevent sheep from wobbling.

Fig. 4

7. Follow manufacturer's instructions to harden compound. Allow to cool. Referring to photo, paint legs white and feet black.
8. Cutting through backing of fabric only, cut ¼" squares from fleece.
9. Leaving face uncovered and working on one small area at a time, use round paintbrush to apply glue to body. Glue wrong sides of fleece squares to sheep; allow to dry.
10. Referring to **Fig. 5**, use liner paintbrush to paint eyes black; paint nose and mouth red. Allow to dry.

Fig. 5

11. Referring to photo, glue ribbon around neck; glue jingle bell to ribbon.

BEESWAX ORNAMENTS
(Shown on page 20)

You will need beeswax; double boiler (or electric frying pan and a can) for melting wax; newspaper; desired cookie cutters (we used a 2¾"h moon and a 2½"w star); square cake pan; vegetable cooking spray; and large, sharp needle and nylon line (for hangers).

1. **Caution: Do not melt wax over an open flame or directly on burner.** Cover work area with newspaper. Melt wax in double boiler over hot water or in a can placed in an electric frying pan filled with water.
2. Spray pan with cooking spray. Pour wax into pan to a depth of approximately ¼". Allow wax to set but not completely harden. Use cookie cutters to cut out desired shapes. Remove shapes from pan.
3. For each hanger, use needle to thread 8" of nylon line through top of ornament. Knot ends of line together.

REDWORK WELCOME PILLOW
(Shown on page 23)

You will need two 9" x 14" pieces and one 1½" x 44" bias strip of white medium weight 50% linen/50% cotton fabric, 44" of ¼" dia. cord, two skeins of red embroidery floss, embroidery hoop, white thread, tracing paper, hot-iron transfer pencil, polyester fiberfill, 1⅜ yds of ⅝"w red grosgrain ribbon, white vinegar, and blocking board and T-pins (optional).

1. Unwrap floss skeins and soak for a few minutes in a mixture of one cup of water and one tablespoon of vinegar. Allow to dry.

2. Trace pattern onto tracing paper. Turn pattern over and use transfer pencil to draw over lines of pattern.

3. With transfer pencil side down, center pattern on one fabric piece; pin in place. Following manufacturer's instructions, transfer design onto fabric.

4. (**Note: Embroidery Stitch Diagrams** are shown on page 158.) Follow Stitch Key and work design using 2 strands of floss.

5. To block stitched piece and remove transfer lines, follow **Blocking Stitched Pieces**, page 156, or have an experienced dry cleaner clean and block the stitched piece.

6. Trim stitched piece and backing fabric to 7½" x 12½".

7. For cording, lay cord along center on wrong side of bias strip. Matching long edges, fold strip over cord. Use zipper foot and machine baste along length of strip close to cord.

8. Matching raw edges and starting 1" from end of cording, baste cording to right side of stitched piece; clip seam allowance at corners. Open ends of cording and cut cord to fit exactly. Insert one end of cording fabric in the other; fold raw edge of top fabric ½" to wrong side and baste in place.

9. For pillow, place stitched piece and backing piece right sides together. Leaving an opening for turning, use zipper foot and sew as close as possible to cording. Cut corners diagonally and turn right side out; press. Stuff pillow with fiberfill and sew final closure by hand.

10. For hanger, cut ribbon in half; referring to photo, sew one end of each length to back of pillow. Tie ends of ribbon together in a bow.

STITCH KEY
- ▨ Satin Stitch
- ◪ Outline Stitch
- ▨ Backstitch
- ◨ Lazy Daisy

REDWORK TABLE RUNNER

(Shown on page 22)

You will need 2/3 yd of 44"w white medium weight 50% linen/50% cotton fabric, 4 skeins of red embroidery floss, white vinegar, embroidery hoop, tracing paper, glue stick, hot-iron transfer pencil, blocking board and T-pins (optional), and white thread.

1. Unwrap floss skeins and soak for a few minutes in a mixture of one cup of water and one tablespoon of vinegar. Allow to dry.

2. Glue tracing paper together to form a 15" x 36" piece. Referring to Diagram, trace scalloped border (in grey) onto tracing paper; trace heart and vine pattern onto tracing paper.

3. Turn pattern over and use transfer pencil to draw over lines of pattern.

4. With transfer pencil side down, center pattern on fabric; pin in place. Following manufacturer's instructions, transfer design onto fabric.

5. (**Note: Embroidery Stitch Diagrams** are shown on page 158.) Follow Stitch Key and work design.

6. To block stitched piece and remove transfer lines, follow **Blocking Stitched Pieces**, page 156, or have an experienced dry cleaner clean and block the stitched piece.

7. Trim fabric to 3" from design.

8. Press edges 1" to wrong side; press edges 1" to wrong side again. Hem table runner.

STITCH KEY

☑ Outline Stitch (2 strands)
☑ Couched Stitching (3 strands)

DIAGRAM

← 1½"

← 1½"

← 1"

36"

15"

A CHRISTMAS HOMECOMING

There's no place like home for the holidays. And no matter where we are, our hearts go home at Christmas to enjoy once again the love and comfort of familiar sights and favorite traditions.

This old-fashioned collection is overflowing with homey decorations that invite us to experience the warmth of a Christmas homecoming. Crowned with a muslin candlewicking star, the tree is adorned with homespun fabric hearts, cross-stitched houses, and folded paper stars. Wooden bead garlands and miniature toy ornaments create an atmosphere of yesteryear, and a candlewicking tree skirt, a companion to the treetop star, surrounds the tree with charm. Scattered about the room, packages wrapped in cheerful plaid paper await eager children on Christmas morning.

Sprays of fresh evergreen and red nandina berries make festive window dressings, while a large homespun heart hung in a doorway welcomes all who pass beneath it. Baskets of poinsettias add a brilliant splash of color.

Instructions for the projects shown here and on the next four pages begin on page 38. Come home for Christmas!

Cross stitched in honor of a family's first Christmas together, our **Hearts Sampler** *(page 44)* will be an heirloom for future generations to treasure.

Topped with a lace-trimmed **Candlewicking Treetop Star** *(page 40)*, the **Christmas Homecoming Tree** *(page 38)* echoes Christmases past. Handmade **Homespun Hearts** *(page 41)* and cross-stitched **House Ornaments** *(page 44)* blend with purchased decorations resembling old-fashioned toys. **Folded Paper Stars** *(page 38)*, patterned after those brought to America by German immigrants, add simplicity to the tree, while red and blue wooden bead garlands spiral about the branches, lending colorful highlights.

We created these ruffled **Homespun Towels** *(page 43)* from bright plaid fabric, borrowing sections from our cross stitch sampler *(shown on opposite page)* and adding warm holiday greetings. A basket of **Homespun Hearts** *(page 41)*, accented with evergreen sprigs, and a **Folded Paper Star** *(page 38)* make a festive arrangement to brighten a corner.

With its star motif and lace edging, the **Candlewicking Tree Skirt** *(page 39)* makes a nice companion to the treetop star.

Easily crafted from homespun fabric, the **Heart Garland** (*page 41*) has a simple charm you'll want to enjoy all year long.

To fashion this hospitable wreath, simply use florist wire to attach fresh greenery and a red velvet bow to a heart-shaped base.

Featuring a cross-stitched house from our **Hearts Sampler** *(page 44)*, this **Photo Album** *(page 43)* is a wonderful place to store Christmas memories.

With a touching table setting of homespun **Heart Place Mats** *(page 41)* and **Heart Napkin Rings** *(page 43)*, holiday meals are sure to warm hearts.

37

CHRISTMAS HOMECOMING TREE
(Shown on page 32)

A fragrant tree decorated with blue homespun fabric and cheery red accents makes every Christmas Homecoming more lovely. Decorations for this 8-foot-tall fresh Frazier fir tree begin at the top with a pieced muslin star embellished with candlewicking, satin stitch, and a dainty lace trim.

The ornaments for the tree are made using several different craft techniques. Echoing the shape of the treetop star, folded paper stars are created from strips of paper. The large, blue heart ornaments are easily sewn and stuffed — a favorite homespun fabric and a topstitched edge make each one special. Four different cross-stitched houses with festive red-checked borders appeal to those who love to stitch. Each design is made into a mini-pillow and hung from the branches with matching grosgrain ribbon. In this section, instructions are included for these ornaments, the treetop star, and the coordinating tree skirt.

Purchased items lend additional charm to the decorations. Loosely twisted together, red and blue wooden bead garlands provide a continuous ribbon of color when wound among the branches. Purchased old-fashioned ornaments — wooden sleds, nutcrackers, miniature doll buggies, and bugles, to name a few — recall toys from Christmases past.

The tree skirt is a pleasing accompaniment for this group of decorations. The treetop star motif is repeated on muslin fabric, and a broad, scalloped edge is enhanced with candlewicking and lace trim. The tree skirt provides a charming backdrop for all the brightly wrapped packages sure to be found at any Christmas Homecoming.

FOLDED PAPER STARS (Shown on page 34)

For each star, you will need one 6" x 20" piece of parchment paper, small scissors or toothpick, and 8" of nylon line (for hanger).

1. Cutting strips very accurately, cut four ¾" x 18" strips of paper.
2. Matching ends, fold each strip in half. Arrange strips as shown in **Fig. 1** and pull ends of strips tightly to form a solid square.

Fig. 1

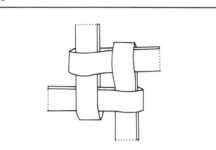

3. (**Note:** For Steps 3 and 4, work with the four strips on top only.) Referring to **Fig. 2a**, fold top left strip down. Rotate one-quarter turn clockwise and repeat until remaining three top strips are folded down, weaving last strip under bottom left square (**Fig. 2b**).

Fig. 2a

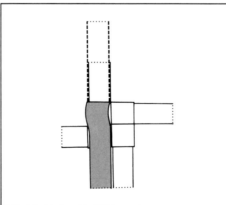

Fig. 2b

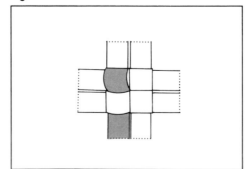

4. Referring to **Fig. 3a**, start with top right strip and fold down and to right. Fold down to form a triangle (**Fig. 3b**). Fold triangle back to left (**Fig. 3c**) and weave end of strip under top right square. Rotate one-quarter turn clockwise and repeat for remaining strips.

Fig. 3a

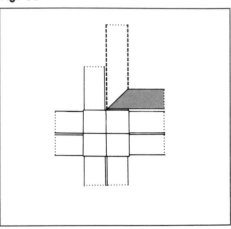

Fig. 3b

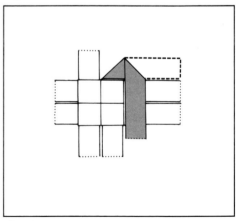

Fig. 3c

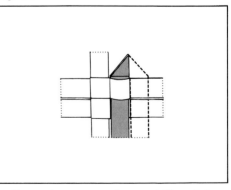

5. Turn star over and repeat Step 4 for bottom strips.
6. To form inner points, hold long strip at upper right up and out of the way to left. Fold bottom right strip up and

FOLDED PAPER STARS (continued)

crease (**Fig. 4a**). Referring to **Fig. 4b**, fold down and to right to form a 45 degree angle; crease strip. Hold the end of strip and turn it counterclockwise, weaving end under upper left square (**Fig. 4c**). Strip will come out through point. Use tip of scissors or toothpick to open point of star to make weaving easier.

Fig. 4a

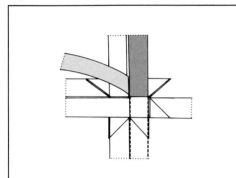

Fig. 4b

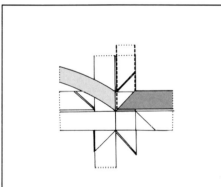

Fig. 4c

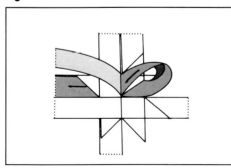

7. Rotate star one-quarter turn clockwise and repeat Step 6 for remaining three top strips.
8. Turn star over and repeat Steps 6 and 7. Trim ends of strips even with outer points of star. For hanger, refer to photo and thread nylon line through section between two outer points of star and knot ends of line together.

CANDLEWICKING TREE SKIRT   (Shown on page 35)

You will need two 60" squares of medium weight unbleached muslin fabric (pieced as necessary), one 60" square of polyester bonded batting, one ball of ecru size 20 cotton crochet thread, removable fabric marking pen, thumbtack or pin, string, hot iron transfer pencil, thread to match fabric, tracing paper, and 5½ yds of ⅜"w ecru lace trim.

1. Fold one fabric square in half from top to bottom and again from left to right.
2. To mark outer guideline, tie one end of string to fabric marking pen. Insert thumbtack through string 27½" from pen. Insert thumbtack in fabric as shown in **Fig. 1** and mark one-fourth of a circle.

Fig. 1

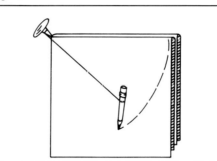

3. To mark inner cutting line, repeat Step 2, inserting thumbtack through string 2" from pen. To mark center of skirt, replace thumbtack with a straight pin.
4. Mark skirt as shown by straight grey line in **Fig. 2**; mark as shown by straight black lines in **Fig. 2**. To mark scallops, insert thumbtack through string 13½" from pen. Refer to **Fig. 2** and insert thumbtack on black line 17" from center mark; mark scallop. Repeat for remaining black line.

Fig. 2

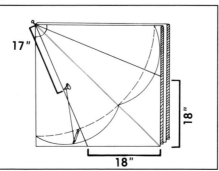

5. Following scalloped and inner cutting lines and cutting through all thicknesses of fabric, cut out skirt. For opening in back of skirt, cut along one fold from outer to inner edge.
6. Use tree skirt star pattern, page 40, and follow **Transferring Patterns**, page 156. Turn pattern over and use transfer pencil to draw over lines and dots of design.
7. With transfer pencil side down, refer to Diagram and position pattern on right side of skirt; pin in place. Following manufacturer's instructions, transfer design onto skirt. Repeat for remaining designs.
8. (**Note:** Mark dots for candlewicking ½" apart.) Refer to Diagram and mark dots 1½" from scalloped edge and along lines dividing sections of skirt.
9. Place skirt and remaining fabric square right sides together on top of batting square. Pin in place. Leaving an opening for turning, sew ½" from raw edge of skirt; using raw edge of skirt as a guide, cut out remaining fabric and batting. Clip curves and cut corners diagonally. Turn right side out; sew final closure by hand. Baste all layers of skirt together.
10. (**Note: Embroidery Stitch Diagrams** are shown on page 158.) Use 1 strand of crochet thread to work Running Stitch along solid lines and 4 strands to work one Colonial Knot at each dot.
11. Remove basting threads and transfer markings. Press skirt on wrong side.
12. Referring to photo, whipstitch lace trim to outer edge of skirt.

DIAGRAM

CANDLEWICKING TREETOP STAR (Shown on page 34)

You will need ½ yd of 44"w medium weight unbleached muslin, 1 yd of ⅜"w ecru lace trim, one 12" x 24" piece of polyester bonded batting, ecru size 20 cotton crochet thread, lightweight cardboard, removable fabric marking pen, dressmaker's carbon, tracing paper, small crochet hook (to turn fabric), and thread to match muslin.

1. Use treetop star pattern and follow **Transferring Patterns,** page 156.
2. For template, use pattern and cut one piece from cardboard.
3. For four **A** pieces, leave at least ½" between pieces and draw around template on muslin four times. Use dressmaker's carbon and pattern to transfer embroidery design to each piece.
4. For four **B** pieces, turn template and pattern over and repeat Step 3.
5. Use fabric marking pen to draw a ¼" seam allowance around each piece; cut out.
6. (**Note:** Match right sides of pieces and use a ¼" seam allowance throughout; press seams open.) For each **AB** section, refer to **Fig. 1** and sew one **A** piece to one **B** piece; repeat for remaining pieces.

Fig. 1

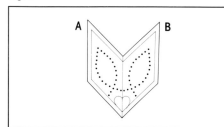

7. For one half of star, refer to **Fig. 2** and sew two **AB** sections together. Repeat to form remaining half.

Fig. 2

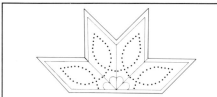

8. Matching points of star pieces, sew halves together.
9. (**Note: Embroidery Stitch Diagrams** are shown on page 158.) Use 4 strands of crochet thread to work one Colonial Knot at each dot on design. Referring to

pattern for direction of stitching, use 2 strands for Satin Stitch at center of design.
10. Remove transfer markings and press star on wrong side.
11. Using star as a pattern, cut two pieces from batting and three pieces from muslin.
12. For front of star, place pieced star and one muslin piece right sides together. Place one batting piece on wrong side of pieced star; sew pieces together. Trim seam allowances and cut corners diagonally. Cut a 3" long slit in lining only and turn star right side out. Use a small crochet hook to turn points. Sew final closure by hand. Press star on wrong side. Repeat for back of star, using remaining muslin and batting pieces.
13. For treetop star opening, refer to photo and leave the area between two points of star open; whipstitch front and back of star together. Referring to photo, whipstitch lace trim to edge of star.

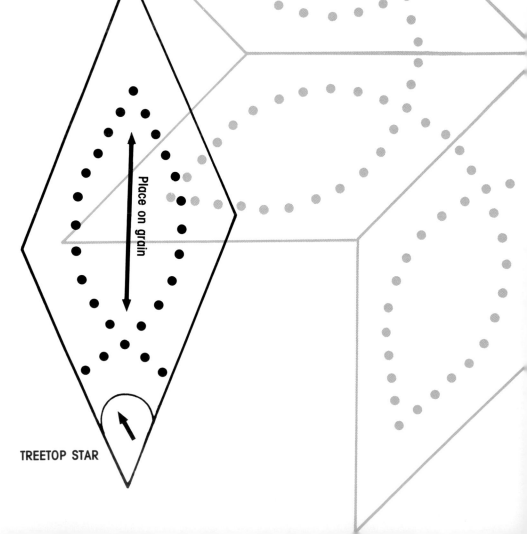

TREE SKIRT STAR

Place on grain

TREETOP STAR

HEART GARLAND
(Shown on page 36)

For an approx. 25" long garland, you will need one 8½"w and two 6"w plastic foam hearts, 1¼ yds of 44"w fabric (use fabric that looks the same on both sides, such as homespun or muslin), and thread to match fabric.

1. For large heart, tear approximately thirty-six 1½" x 13½" strips from fabric. Matching ends, fold one strip in half; refer to **Fig. 1** to knot strip around heart. Repeat with remaining strips.

Fig. 1

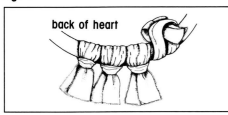
back of heart

2. For each small heart, repeat Step 1, tearing approximately thirty 1" x 10" strips from fabric.
3. To assemble garland, tear two 1½" x 3" fabric pieces. Refer to photo for position of hearts. On backs of hearts, whipstitch short edges of one fabric piece to large heart and one small heart. Repeat to attach remaining small heart.
4. For hanging strips, tear two fabric strips 2" wide and desired length. Refer to photo and whipstitch ends of strips to ends of garland.

HOMESPUN HEARTS
(Shown on pages 32 and 34)

You will need two 8" squares of fabric for each tree heart or two 10" squares of fabric for each door heart, thread to match fabric, polyester fiberfill, tracing paper, fabric marking pencil, crochet hook (to turn fabric), and 8" of nylon line (for door heart hanger).

1. Use tree heart or door heart pattern, page 42, and follow **Transferring Patterns** and **Sewing Shapes**, page 156, to make each heart. Lightly stuff each heart with fiberfill; sew final closure by hand.
2. Topstitch ¼" from edge of each heart.
3. For door heart hanger, thread nylon line through top center of heart; knot ends of line together.

HEART PLACE MATS (Shown on page 37)

For each place mat, you will need one 1½" x 60" bias strip (pieced if necessary) and two 22" x 16" pieces of fabric, one 22" x 16" piece of polyester bonded batting, thread to match fabric, embroidery floss, transparent tape, and tracing paper.

1. Use place mat top and bottom patterns, page 42, and follow **Transferring Patterns**, page 156. Matching arrows to form one pattern, tape patterns together.
2. Use pattern and cut two place mat pieces from fabric and one place mat piece from batting.
3. Place one fabric piece right side down. Place batting and remaining fabric piece right side up on fabric piece. Baste layers together.
4. For binding, match wrong sides and raw edges and fold bias strip in half lengthwise; press. Fold long raw edges to center; press.
5. To apply binding, open one end of binding; press end ¼" to wrong side. Unfold one long edge of binding. Matching right sides and raw edges, place pressed end of binding along left side of place mat, 2" from bottom point (**Fig. 1**). Pin binding to edge of place mat, continuing clockwise around to bottom point of place mat.

Fig. 1

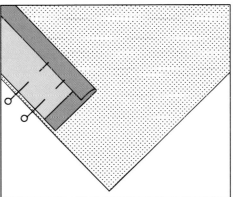

6. Using a ⅜" seam allowance, stitch binding to place mat to within ⅜" of bottom point (**Fig. 2a**). Fold binding at bottom point as shown in **Fig. 2b**. Pin binding to remaining edge of place mat and overlap ends ½"; cut off excess. Beginning at bottom right edge of place mat, stitch remaining binding in place (**Fig. 2c**).

Fig. 2a

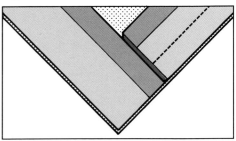

Fig. 2b

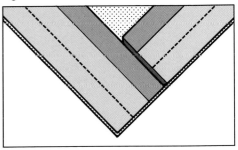

Fig. 2c

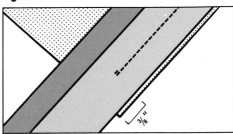

7. Fold binding over raw edges to back of place mat; whipstitch binding in place.
8. To tie layers together, refer to **Fig. 3** and use 8" of floss for each tie. On front of place mat, go down through place mat at one **x**; come up approximately ⅛" away. Securely knot floss close to fabric; trim ends to approximately ¾". Repeat for remaining **x**'s. Remove basting threads.

Fig. 3

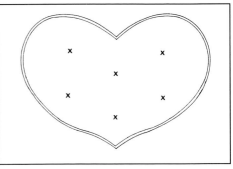

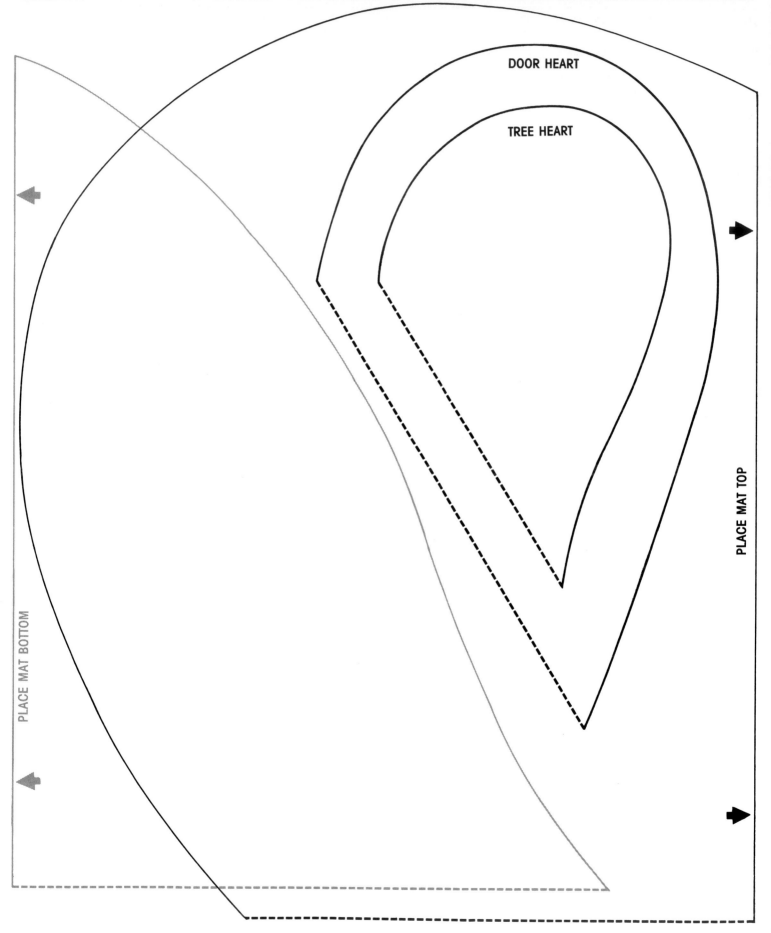

DOOR HEART

TREE HEART

PLACE MAT TOP

PLACE MAT BOTTOM

PHOTO ALBUM (Shown on page 37)

You will need photo album (we used a 10" x 11½" album), fabric to cover album (with album opened flat, fabric should be 2" larger than album on all sides), ⅝"w grosgrain ribbon, thread to match ribbon, one 6" x 6½" piece of Fiddler's Lite (14 ct), embroidery floss (see color key, page 44), embroidery hoop (optional), lightweight fusible interfacing, paper-backed fusible web, grid paper for charting name and date, and fabric glue.

1. Use 2 strands of floss for Cross Stitch. With top of border ¾" from one short edge of Fiddler's Lite, work one house with border from Hearts Sampler, page 44. Referring to photo, use alphabet and numbers at bottom of chart to chart name, "EST." and the year, and one heart on grid paper. Center and stitch name, date, and heart below house, leaving 2 fabric threads between bottom of border and lettering and between each line of lettering.
2. Cut interfacing slightly smaller than album cover fabric and stitched piece. Follow manufacturer's instructions to fuse interfacing to wrong sides of fabric and stitched piece.
3. For album cover, wrap fabric around album and use a pin to mark center front of album on fabric.
4. Use web and follow manufacturer's instructions to fuse stitched piece to center front of album cover.
5. Refer to photo and **Fig. 1a** to glue ribbon around edge of stitched piece, mitering ribbon at each corner (**Fig. 1b**). Stitch close to inside and outside edges of ribbon.

Fig. 1a

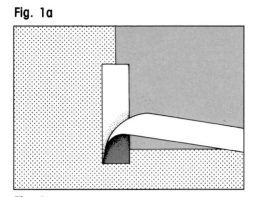

Fig. 1b

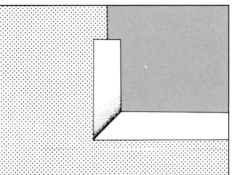

6. Cut two lengths of ribbon the same length as short edges of album cover fabric. Glue ribbon lengths over short edges on right side of fabric; allow to dry. Press long edges of fabric 1" to wrong side.
7. Place album cover fabric wrong side up on a flat surface. Open album and center on fabric. Sliding center of folded edge under binding ring hardware, fold top edge of cover fabric over top edge of album; glue to secure. Repeat for bottom edge. Fold short edges of cover over side edges of album and glue to secure. Allow to dry.

HOMESPUN TOWELS
(Shown on page 35)

For each towel, you will need one 13" x 18" and one 26" x 4" piece of fabric for towel, thread to match fabric, one 13" x 4⅜" piece of Fiddler's II Lite (18 ct), embroidery floss (see color key, page 44), embroidery hoop (optional), and grid paper for charting greeting.

1. Use 2 strands of floss for Cross Stitch. With top of design ⅞" from one long edge of Fiddler's II Lite, work one house without border from Hearts Sampler, page 44. Referring to photo, use alphabet at bottom of chart to chart desired greeting on grid paper. With tops of letters 5 fabric threads below bottom of house design, center and stitch greeting below house design.
2. With right sides together, match top edge of stitched piece with one short edge of 13" x 18" fabric piece. Using a ½" seam allowance, sew fabric and stitched piece together; press seam allowance toward fabric.
3. With wrong sides together, fold 26" x 4" fabric piece in half lengthwise and press. Baste ½" and ¼" from long raw edge. Pull basting threads, gathering fabric to fit bottom edge of stitched piece.
4. Matching right sides and raw edges, pin ruffle to bottom edge of stitched piece. Using a ½" seam allowance, sew ruffle and stitched piece together. Press seam allowance toward stitched piece.
5. Press long edges of towel ¼" to wrong side; press ¼" to wrong side again and hem. Press remaining raw edge ¼" to wrong side; press ½" to wrong side again and hem.

HEART NAPKIN RINGS (Shown on page 37)

For each napkin ring, you will need self-hardening clay, ivory and blue acrylic paint, walnut water-based stain, paintbrushes, matte clear acrylic spray, rolling pin, waxed paper, paring knife, tracing paper, and a soft cloth.

1. Trace heart pattern onto tracing paper and cut out.
2. On waxed paper, roll out a ⅛" thick piece of clay approximately 5" x 6". Place pattern on clay and use knife to cut around heart; cut a 1¼" x 5½" strip from clay. Carefully lift pieces from

paper. Use fingers to smooth edges of heart and strip. Overlap short edges of strip to form a 1½" dia. ring, smoothing overlapped area.
3. To join heart and ring, brush one side of heart and overlapped area of ring with water. Referring to photo, press heart on ring. Slightly flatten ring into an oval shape; allow to dry.
4. Paint ring ivory and heart blue; allow to dry. Apply stain and remove excess with soft cloth; allow to dry.
5. Spray napkin ring with acrylic spray.

NAPKIN RING HEART

HEARTS SAMPLER

(Shown on page 34)

You will need one 15" square of Fiddler's Lite (14 ct), embroidery floss (see color key), embroidery hoop, grid paper for charting name and date, and desired frame (we used a custom frame).

1. Work design on fabric, using 2 strands of floss for Cross Stitch. Referring to photo, use alphabet and numbers at bottom of chart to chart name, heart, and "EST." and the year on grid paper. Center and stitch name and date where indicated on chart.
2. Frame as desired.

HOUSE ORNAMENTS

(Shown on page 34)

For each ornament, you will need 24" of ⅜"w red grosgrain ribbon, two 8" squares of Fiddler's Lite (14 ct), embroidery floss (see color key), embroidery hoop (optional), polyester fiberfill, and thread to match fabric.

1. Using 2 strands of floss for Cross Stitch, work one house design with border from Hearts Sampler on one fabric square.
2. Trim fabric to 1" from design. Using stitched piece as a pattern, cut out remaining fabric square. Cut ribbon in half. Pin ribbon pieces on front of stitched piece ½" above top of stitched design (**Fig. 1**).

Fig. 1

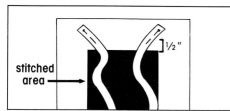

3. (**Note:** Use a ½" seam allowance.) Place stitched piece and remaining fabric square right sides together. Leaving an opening for turning and being careful not to catch loose ribbon ends in stitching, sew pieces together.
4. Trim seam allowance and cut corners diagonally; turn right side out and press. Stuff ornament with fiberfill; sew final closure by hand.
5. Tie ribbon ends in a bow and trim ends.

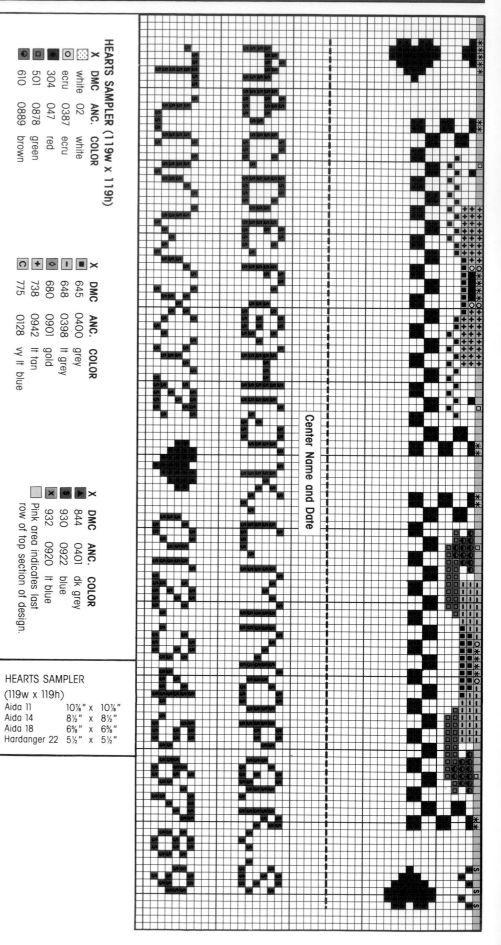

HEARTS SAMPLER (119w x 119h)

X	DMC	ANC.	COLOR
	white	02	white
	ecru	0387	ecru
	304	047	red
	501	0878	green
	610	0889	brown

X	DMC	ANC.	COLOR
	645	0400	grey
	648	0398	lt grey
	680	0901	gold
	738	0942	lt tan
	775	0128	vy lt blue

Pink area indicates last row of top section of design.

X	DMC	ANC.	COLOR
	844	0401	dk grey
	930	0922	blue
	932	0920	lt blue

Center Name and Date

HEARTS SAMPLER

(119w x 119h)

Aida 11	10⅞" x	10⅞"
Aida 14	8½" x	8½"
Aida 18	6⅝" x	6⅝"
Hardanger 22	5½" x	5½"

When courageous settlers traveled westward, the spirit of Christmas followed. And as the great Southwest was tamed, the customs of American frontiersmen and Spanish missionaries merged with those of the native Indians to produce a heritage rich in rustic beauty. Inspired by the work of the area's artisans, we borrowed colors from the Painted Desert to create a special holiday collection filled with symbols of the season.

Beneath a silvery treetop star, raffia angels proclaim the good news of the Savior's birth. Pastel cross ornaments inspire thoughts of the messages shared in little adobe missions, and glass balls are given a stucco-like texture and painted to resemble Indian pottery. Strands of lights enhanced with silver conchas give off a soft glow, reflected by shiny mirrored ornaments. Spiky gum ball ''stars'' add a natural touch. To complete the mood, glowing candles and luminarias are placed throughout the house, and a tumbleweed is adorned with cutout paper ornaments that have the look of aged copper.

Instructions for the projects shown here and on the next four pages begin on page 52. With our innovative craft techniques, you can bring the beauty of the Southwest into your home this Christmas!

Sun-washed shades of turquoise and rose mingle with silver and natural colors on the **Southwest Celebration Tree** *(page 52)*. **Raffia Angels** *(page 57)* rest among the branches beneath a **Tin Treetop Star** *(page 55)*; a light dusting of spray paint gives the star the appearance of weathered silver. Soft-colored **Stucco Ball Ornaments** *(page 55)* provide a delicate contrast to rustic gum ball stars, while ornately shaped **Cross Ornaments** *(page 58)* recall the influence of Spanish missionaries. Trimmed with pastel raffia braids, **Mirrored Ornaments** *(page 52)* reflect the amber glow of **Concha Lights** *(page 54)*, and purchased garlands of woven straw and mesh ribbon wrap the tree in Southwest charm.

Reminiscent of the Star of Bethlehem and the angels who heralded Christ's birth, a **Tin Treetop Star** *(page 55)* and a pair of large **Raffia Angels** *(page 57)* make a lovely accent for a shelf. Swirls of mesh ribbon unify the arrangement.

(*Far left*) A graceful grouping of handcrafted **Candlesticks** (*page 52*) makes an attractive focal point for a table. Pale pink tapers accentuate the handsome blue-green patina, which is created with a simple painting technique.

A pretty wreath trimmed with **Verdigris Paper Ornaments** (*page 53*) is filled with symbols of the peace and joy of the season.

The subtly shaded pattern on our Tree Skirt (*page 54*) is created by using a variation of huck embroidery on evenweave Monk's Cloth. Echoing the colors of the skirt, packages wrapped in hand-painted **Gift Wrap** (*page 56*) are tied with raffia bows, and colorful mesh ribbon dresses up plain wrapping paper.

Inspired by the candle-lit paper lanterns brought to the Southwest by Mexican settlers, our sturdy **Tin Luminarias** *(page 56)* have a punched sunburst design.

Nestled in **Tin Candle Holders** *(page 58)*, plain white candles enhance the beauty of the simple setting. The round holders feature scalloped and pointed edges, while the square holder displays a distinctive adobe step silhouette.

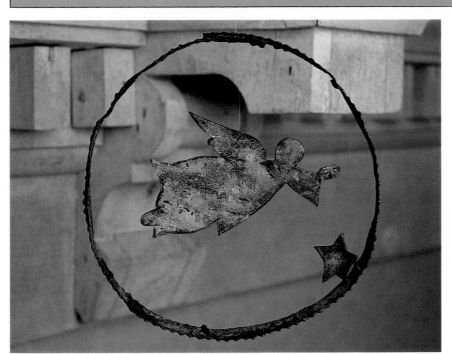

Bearing ''good tidings of great joy,'' the heavenly messenger in this mobile of **Verdigris Paper Ornaments** *(page 53)* reminds us of the very first Christmas.

Verdigris Paper Ornaments *(page 53)* in the shapes of angels, doves, Christmas trees, and stars have the look of antique copper — but they're really inexpensive to create with paper, glue, and paint! Here they adorn a tumbleweed, but these unusual ornaments will add beauty to any type of tree. To hold our tumbleweed, we gave a clay pot a weathered copper look by using the painting technique for our **Candlesticks** *(page 52)*.

SOUTHWEST CELEBRATION TREE

(Shown on page 46)

Bring a taste of the Southwest to Christmas festivities by decorating your tree with the soft pastels of the Painted Desert. Inexpensive items such as foam meat trays, old glass Christmas balls, and raffia make the job easy and affordable.

Only a couple of purchased items are used as accents for all the handmade decorations. A purchased woven straw garland resembling large beads adorns the branches, while 3" wide mesh ribbon called Sinamay or angel hair ribbon falls in gentle twists and curves. Even the miniature white tree lights offer a handcrafted touch — a concha surrounding each light makes them glow more brightly.

The purchased garlands highlight the natural-colored raffia used to make the angels that sit among the branches. With dresses of pink or turquoise raffia, the flowing gowns of these native angels add instant drama to the tree.

Other ornaments add a distinctive Southwest flavor to the decorations. Old glass Christmas balls become new again when a stucco finish in pale pink is applied. Spanish-inspired crosses look like imports from Santa Fe, but are in fact made from foam meat trays found at the local grocer's. Mirrors to reflect the rising sun are set in diamond-shaped ornaments cut from aluminum flashing. Instructions for the concha lights and these ornaments are included in this section.

The last ornaments added to the tree — the prickly gum ball stars — need no instructions at all. Round toothpicks are glued into the openings of sweet gum balls and a coat of glossy wood tone spray gives the stars a natural color.

Aluminum flashing is also used to create the glorious treetop star. When cut, rolled, crimped, and set off with a small mirror, this silvery showpiece belies its humble beginnings. To complete the decorative theme, a deeply fringed square of Monk's Cloth makes a lovely tree skirt when highlighted with a huck-embroidered design in pink and turquoise.

With instructions to help you every step of the way, now is the time to bring a Southwest Celebration into your home for Christmas.

CANDLESTICKS (Shown on page 49)

For each 9", 11", or 13" candlestick, you will need one 5"h metal funnel with a 4" dia. opening; one 3"h metal funnel with a 2¾" dia. opening; three 1" dia. wooden beads with ⅜" dia. openings; one 5", 7", or 9" length of ⅜" dia. dowel; gesso; foam brushes; small pieces of cellulose sponge; hot glue gun; glue sticks; hacksaw; and black, lt turquoise, turquoise, dk turquoise, and white acrylic paint.

1. Refer to **Fig. 1** and use hacksaw to cut small end from each funnel.

Fig. 1

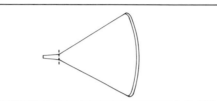

2. For base, place one bead on dowel ½" from one end; glue to secure. Insert remaining end of dowel through large opening of 5" funnel (**Fig. 2a**). Place another bead on dowel; glue bead at small end of funnel (**Fig. 2b**).

Fig. 2a   **Fig. 2b**

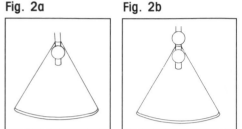

3. With tops of bead and dowel even, place remaining bead on dowel; glue to secure. Refer to photo and glue small end of 3" funnel to bead.
4. Apply two coats of gesso, then two coats of black paint to candlestick, allowing to dry between coats.
5. Dampen sponge pieces and squeeze out excess water.
6. Referring to photo, use sponge pieces and a stamping motion to paint candlestick with dk turquoise paint, allowing some black to show through. Repeat with turquoise, lt turquoise, and white paint.

MIRRORED ORNAMENTS (Shown on page 48)

For each ornament, you will need one 4" x 6" piece of aluminum flashing (available at hardware stores), awl or ice pick, hammer, utility scissors, tracing paper, 3 different-colored strands of raffia, standard screwdriver with ¼"w blade, scrap piece of soft wood, 1¾" x 2½" diamond-shaped mirror, hot glue gun, and glue sticks.

1. (**Note:** Cut edges of flashing may be sharp.) Trace ornament pattern onto tracing paper and cut out. Use pattern and utility scissors to cut ornament from flashing.
2. Place ornament on wood. Use awl and hammer to punch holes where indicated by dots on pattern. Use screwdriver and hammer to score ornament where indicated by blue lines on pattern.
3. Glue mirror to center of ornament.
4. Knot raffia strands together 1" from one end. Braid raffia to fit around edge of mirror (approximately 6½") and knot remaining end. Trim ends ½" from each knot. Referring to photo, glue raffia braid around edge of mirror.
5. For hanger, thread 9" of raffia through hole in top of ornament. Knot ends of raffia together ½" from top of ornament; knot again ½" from ends.

top

VERDIGRIS PAPER ORNAMENTS (Shown on pages 49 and 51)

You will need Aleene's "Tacky" Glue; brown craft paper or brown paper bag; tracing paper; needle nose pliers or tweezers; lt blue, turquoise, and white acrylic paint; Spanish Copper Rub 'n Buff® metallic finish; foam brush; candle in holder; a soft cloth; matte clear acrylic spray; and nylon line (for hangers).

For angel mobile, you will also need pinking shears, hot glue gun, and glue sticks.

For wreath, you will also need one 10" dia. metal ring, black spray paint, hot glue gun, and glue sticks.

ORNAMENTS

1. (**Note:** For flying angel ornament, use flying angel and small star patterns. For three-star ornament, use large, medium, and small star patterns. For tree ornament, use tree and small star patterns.) Trace desired patterns onto tracing paper and cut out.

2. (**Note:** Follow Steps 2 — 9 for each ornament shape.) Cut five pieces of craft paper 1" larger on all sides than pattern.

3. Mix 1 part water to 1 part glue. Working quickly, apply a thin coat of diluted glue to four of the pieces of craft paper; place all five pieces together. Do not allow to dry.

4. Use pattern and cut out shape.

5. (**Caution:** Use extreme care when working over open candle flame. To avoid burns, use pliers to hold shape over flame.) Light candle. Apply a thick coat of undiluted glue to one side of shape. Place wet glue directly into candle flame. Move shape through flame until all the glue has burned to a solid black color. If parts of shape look brown, continue burning until glue turns completely black. Repeat for remaining side of shape. Allow to cool.

6. Use soft cloth to wipe excess black soot from shape.

7. To paint shape, refer to photo and use finger to rub a small amount of one color of paint onto each side of shape. Overlapping some areas of paint and leaving some of the shape unpainted, repeat with remaining colors. Allow to dry.

8. Refer to photo and use finger to lightly rub a small amount of Rub 'n Buff® onto each side of shape, leaving recessed areas untouched.

9. Lightly spray shape with acrylic spray; allow to dry.

10. For flying angel ornament, refer to photo and use nylon line to hang small star 1½" from angel's hand. For three-star ornament, refer to photo and hang medium star 1¼" from large star; hang small star ¾" from medium star. For tree ornament, refer to photo and glue star to tree.

11. For hangers, thread 6" of nylon line through top of each ornament and knot ends of line together.

ANGEL MOBILE

1. Trace flying angel and small star patterns onto tracing paper and cut out. For ring strip pattern, cut a ¾" x 22" piece of tracing paper.

2. Using pinking shears to cut out ring strip, follow Steps 2 — 9 of Ornaments instructions to make angel, star, and ring strip.

3. To form ring, overlap short ends of ring strip 1¼" and hot glue to secure. Referring to photo, use nylon line to hang star 1½" from angel's hand; hang angel 2" from top of ring.

4. For hanger, thread desired length of nylon line through top of ring and knot ends of line together.

WREATH

1. Trace flying angel, standing angel, dove, large star, and medium star patterns onto tracing paper and cut out.

2. Burning and painting one side of each shape only, follow Steps 2 — 9 of Ornaments instructions to make two shapes from each pattern.

3. Spray paint ring; allow to dry. To paint ring, follow Steps 7 — 9 of Ornaments instructions.

4. Referring to photo, hot glue shapes to ring.

53

TREE SKIRT (Shown on page 49)

You will need one 51" square of Monk's Cloth (7 count), tapestry yarn or sport weight knitting yarn (see color key), Stole weaving needle or yarn needle, compass, fabric marking pencil, and thread to match fabric.

1. Use straight pins to mark center of fabric and center of each edge of fabric.

2. Thread needle with a 2½ yd length of turquoise yarn. Referring to Diagram and Stitching Technique (**Fig. 1**), follow chart to stitch half of first row of design; work end of yarn straight to edge of fabric. Stitch remaining half of first row. Following chart, stitch remaining rows of design.

3. Repeat Step 2 for each edge of fabric.

4. To fringe fabric, refer to Diagram and machine stitch 5" from each edge; remove fabric threads up to machine-stitched line.

5. Referring to Diagram, use compass to mark a 3" dia. circle at center of fabric; use fabric marking pencil to mark opening.

6. Stitch ¼" from pencil lines. Cut fabric on pencil lines.

7. Press raw edges ¼" to wrong side; press ¼" to wrong side again and hem.

DIAGRAM

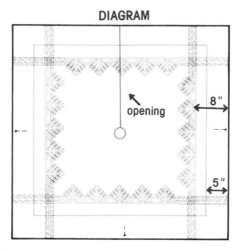

opening

8"

5"

STITCHING TECHNIQUE

Match center of design to center of stitching area. Follow **Fig. 1** for stitching technique, weaving yarn under vertical fabric threads. Begin working the first (bottom) row at the center by threading needle with yarn and slipping it under the center vertical fabric thread; draw half of yarn through. Leaving remaining yarn at center, work half of the design from center to edge of fabric. Turn work upside down; rethread needle with remaining thread end and stitch remaining half of first row. Remaining rows may be worked completely from right to left or from left to right.

Fig. 1

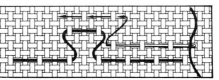

CONCHA LIGHTS

(Shown on page 48)

For a 50-bulb string of white miniature tree lights, you will need fifty 1½" dia. conchas, wire cutters, and green florist clay (optional).

1. For each light, refer to **Fig. 1a** and use wire cutters to cut through center of crossbar on one concha. Bend each half of crossbar to back of concha (**Fig. 1b**).

Fig. 1a

Fig. 1b

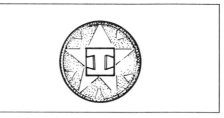

2. Insert light through concha from front to back so concha cups around light. Squeeze halves of crossbar tightly around base of light to secure. If desired, use florist clay to secure concha to light.

TREE SKIRT

- ✔ lt pink — 30 yds
- ✔ pink — 20 yds
- ✔ lt turquoise — 10 yds
- ✔ turquoise — 10 yds

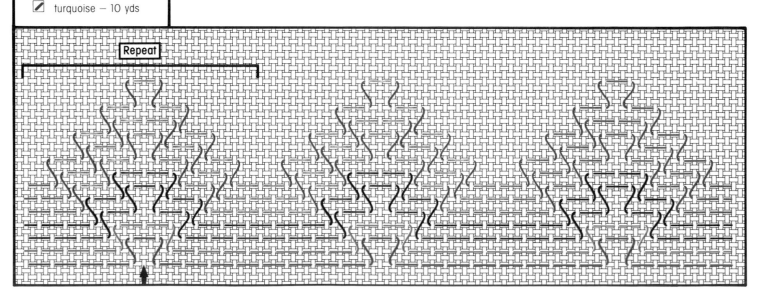

Repeat

TIN TREETOP STAR (Shown on page 48)

You will need one 14" x 17" piece of aluminum flashing (available at hardware stores), utility scissors, one 4" dia. metal ring, needle nose pliers, 1" dia. mirror, flat grey and flat black spray paint, fine steel wool, hot glue gun, glue sticks, ruler, tracing paper, and small piece of florist wire.

1. Trace large point and small point patterns onto tracing paper and cut out. For circle patterns, draw one 2½" dia. and one 2" dia. circle onto tracing paper and cut out.
2. (**Note:** Cut edges of flashing may be sharp.) Use patterns and utility scissors to cut five large points, five small points, one large circle, and one small circle from flashing.
3. Referring to photo and patterns, use pliers to crimp edge of small circle and long edges of all point pieces.
4. Refer to **Figs. 1a** and **1b** and use pliers to curl uncrimped edges of each large point.

Fig. 1a

Fig. 1b

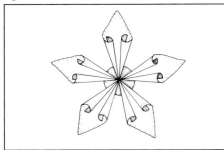

5. Center ruler lengthwise on one small point and fold flashing up against ruler to form an approximately 45 degree angle. Repeat for remaining small points.
6. Place large points on large circle as shown in **Fig. 2**; glue to secure.

Fig. 2

7. Referring to photo and **Fig. 3**, glue small points between large points.

Fig. 3

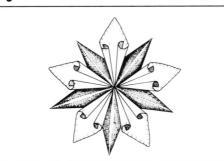

8. Glue metal ring in center on back of star.
9. Glue remaining circle to center front of star.
10. Lightly spray front of star with grey paint; allow to dry. Keeping paint can about 12" away, lightly spray star with black paint; allow to dry. Use steel wool to remove some of the paint in several places on star.
11. Glue mirror to center front of star.
12. Wire star to top of tree.

STUCCO BALL ORNAMENTS
(Shown on page 48)

You will need desired size glass ball ornaments, DecoArt™ Snow-Tex™ textural medium, pink acrylic paint, gesso, rose and turquoise iridescent squeezable fabric paint pens, foam brushes, and Design Master® glossy wood tone spray (available at craft stores).

1. Apply one coat of gesso to balls; allow to dry.
2. Mix 1 teaspoon acrylic paint to 4 tablespoons Snow-Tex™. Mixing more paint and Snow-Tex™ as needed, apply one coat of mixture to balls; allow to dry.
3. Referring to photo, use one paint pen to paint wavy line around center of each ball; use remaining pen to paint dots. Allow to dry.
4. Lightly spray balls with wood tone spray; allow to dry.

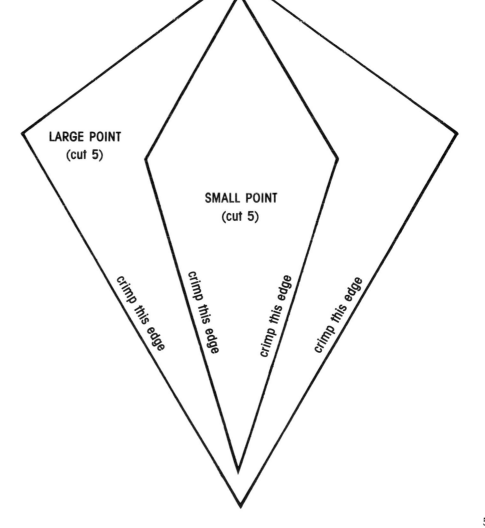

LARGE POINT
(cut 5)

SMALL POINT
(cut 5)

crimp this edge

crimp this edge

crimp this edge

crimp this edge

GIFT WRAP
(Shown on page 49)

You will need wrapping paper, 6" x 3½" x 1" cellulose sponges, tracing paper, foam brushes, round paintbrush, and desired colors of acrylic paint.

1. Use desired gift wrap patterns and follow **Transferring Patterns**, page 156. Use patterns and cut shapes from sponges.
2. Dampen sponge shapes and squeeze out excess water. Use foam brush to apply an even coat of paint to sponge shapes. Reapplying paint as needed, stamp desired shapes on wrapping paper. Allow to dry.
3. Use round paintbrush to paint lines on wrapping paper. Allow to dry.

TIN LUMINARIAS (Shown on page 50)

For each luminaria, you will need aluminum flashing (available at hardware stores), utility scissors, awl or ice pick, scrap piece of soft wood, hammer, ruler, old pair of pinking shears, flat grey and flat black spray paint, pencil, tracing paper, transparent tape, sandpaper, hot glue gun, and glue sticks.

1. (**Note:** Cut edges of flashing may be sharp.) Using pinking shears to cut one long edge (top) and utility scissors to cut remaining edges, cut flashing the following size:

    small luminaria — 6¾" x 16½"
    medium luminaria — 8½" x 16½"
    large luminaria — 9½" x 16½"

2. Refer to **Fig. 1** and use pencil to mark lines on one side (front) of flashing.

Fig. 1

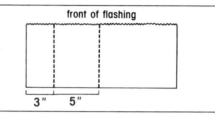

front of flashing

3"   5"

3. Trace sunburst pattern onto tracing paper.
4. Center pattern on 5" section of flashing and tape in place. Place 5" section of flashing on wood. Use awl and hammer to punch holes in flashing where indicated by dots on pattern. Remove pattern.
5. Lightly spray front of flashing with grey paint; allow to dry. Keeping paint can about 12" away, lightly spray flashing with black paint; allow to dry.
6. Refer to **Fig. 2** and use pencil to mark lines on back of flashing. Place ruler against each line and bend flashing to form a box.

Fig. 2

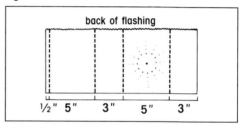

back of flashing

½" 5"   3"   5"   3"

7. Referring to photo, crease side sections lengthwise to resemble a paper bag.
8. Sand ½" wide section. Overlap short edges of luminaria; glue to secure.

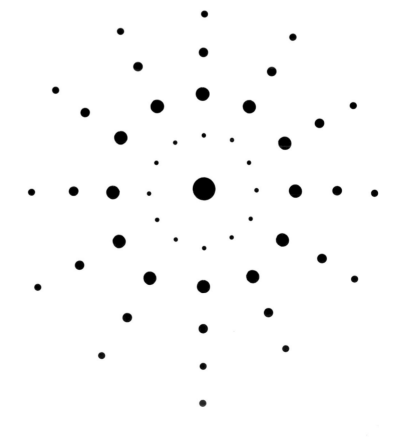

RAFFIA ANGELS (Shown on pages 46 and 48)

Note: Instructions are written for small angel with sizes for large angel in parentheses.

For each angel, you will need one bundle of natural raffia at least 40" (60") long and approx. 2" (4") in circumference (to measure circumference, wrap a tape measure around bundle of raffia), one bundle of desired color raffia at least 28" (48") long and approx. 1" (2") in circumference for dress, heavy thread (buttonhole twist) to match natural raffia, natural Paper Capers™ twisted paper, one 1½" (1¾") dia. wooden ball knob, tracing paper, hot glue gun, glue sticks, jute, and small amount of dried flowers.

For halo, you will need supplies listed in Cross Ornaments instructions, page 58 (omit nylon line).

1. (**Note:** For best results, use raffia strands no wider than ⅛"; raffia will easily separate into narrower widths.) For head, pull a 1" (2") thick section of natural raffia from bundle. Use thread to tie strands together at centers. Refer to **Fig. 1a** and place strands on one side of thread tie over top of knob. Refer to **Fig. 1b** and fold remaining strands over knob and smooth down.

Fig. 1a

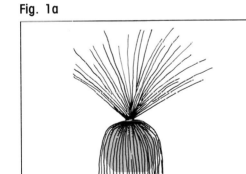

Fig. 1b

2. For neck, use thread and tie raffia strands together below knob (**Fig. 2**).

Fig. 2

3. For dress, pull a 1" (2") thick section of colored raffia from bundle. Place centers of strands evenly around neck and use thread to securely tie strands together (**Fig. 3**). Fold raffia over thread and smooth down. Mark center front of dress.

Fig. 3

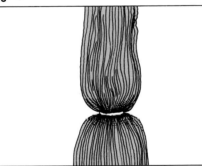

4. For sleeves, refer to **Fig. 4** and separate 30 (40) strands of colored raffia from each side of dress; use thread to tie strands together 3" (4") from neck.

Fig. 4

5. For arms, cut one 8½" (10") length of twisted paper and untwist; fold in half lengthwise. For hands, twist paper together at center. With hands at center front of dress, glue short edges of paper at center back below neck (**Fig. 5**).

Fig. 5

6. Glue thread ties of sleeves at back of angel below arms.

7. Trace wing pattern onto tracing paper and cut out. Cut one 17" length of twisted paper and untwist. Use pattern and cut two wings from paper. Refer to photo and glue wings to back of angel.

8. For hair, pull a 1" (2") thick section of natural raffia from bundle. Use thread to tie strands together at centers. Place strands on one side of thread tie evenly over top center of head; glue in place at knot. Fold remaining strands over head and smooth down. Refer to photo and arrange hair as desired; glue in place.

9. For halo, use small or large halo pattern, page 59, and follow Steps 1 – 5 of Cross Ornaments instructions, page 58. Refer to photo and glue halo to head.

10. For bouquet, refer to photo and use jute to tie dried flowers to hands.

WING (cut 2)

TIN CANDLE HOLDERS (Shown on page 50)

For each square holder, you will need one 2¼" x 10⅜" and one 2½" x 3½" piece of aluminum flashing (available at hardware stores), pencil, ruler, standard screwdriver with ¼"w blade, hot glue gun, and glue sticks.

For each scalloped or sunburst holder, you will need one 6" square of aluminum flashing (available at hardware stores), silver squeezable fabric paint pen, and a standard screwdriver with ¼"w blade (for sunburst holder only).

You will also need utility scissors, awl or ice pick, hammer, scrap piece of soft wood, and tracing paper.

SQUARE HOLDER

1. Use square holder pattern and follow **Transferring Patterns**, page 156.
2. Refer to **Fig. 1** and use pencil to mark lines on one side (back) of 2¼" x 10⅜" piece of flashing.

Fig. 1

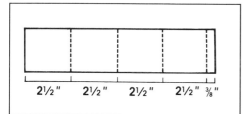

| 2½" | 2½" | 2½" | 2½" | ⅜" |

3. (**Note:** Cut edges of flashing may be sharp.) On each 2½" wide section of flashing, use pencil to draw around black lines on pattern. Use utility scissors to cut out holder on black lines.
4. Place holder on wood. On front of holder, use awl and hammer to punch holes where indicated by black dots on pattern. Use screwdriver and hammer to score holder where indicated by blue lines on pattern.
5. On back of holder, place ruler against each pencil line and bend holder to form a box. Overlap short edges; glue to secure.
6. For bottom of holder, use pencil to draw a line ½" from each short edge of 2½" x 3½" piece of flashing. Place ruler against each line and bend flashing up. Insert bottom into holder; glue to secure.

SCALLOPED OR SUNBURST HOLDER

1. (**Note:** Cut edges of flashing may be sharp.) Use scalloped or sunburst holder pattern and follow **Transferring**

Patterns, page 156. Use pattern and utility scissors to cut holder from flashing.
2. Place holder on wood. Use awl and hammer to punch holes where indicated by black dots on pattern. For sunburst holder, use screwdriver and hammer to score holder where indicated by blue lines on pattern.
3. Use paint pen to paint lines where indicated by grey lines on pattern. Allow to dry.
4. Referring to photo, bend edges of holder where indicated by grey dotted lines on pattern.

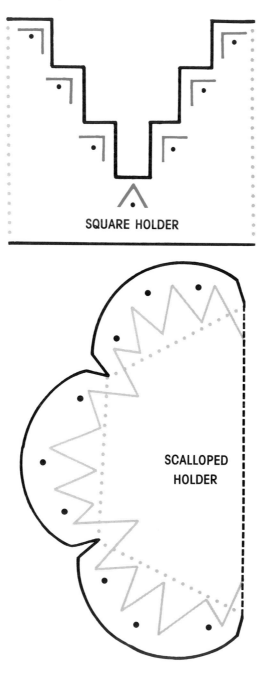

SQUARE HOLDER

SCALLOPED HOLDER

CROSS ORNAMENTS

(Shown on page 48)

For each ornament, you will need one 6½" x 9" foam meat tray (available in meat department of grocery store), tracing paper, gesso, craft knife, foam brush, small round paintbrush, graphite transfer paper, Design Master™ glossy wood tone spray (available at craft stores), desired colors of acrylic paint, and 8" of nylon line (for hanger).

1. Use desired cross pattern, page 59, and follow **Transferring Patterns**, page 156.
2. Use transfer paper and a dull pencil to transfer pattern onto smooth side of meat tray; use craft knife to cut out.
3. Apply two coats of gesso to front and back of ornament, allowing to dry between coats.
4. Referring to photo, paint front and back of ornament; allow to dry.
5. Lightly spray ornament with wood tone spray.
6. For hanger, thread nylon line through top of ornament; knot ends of line together.

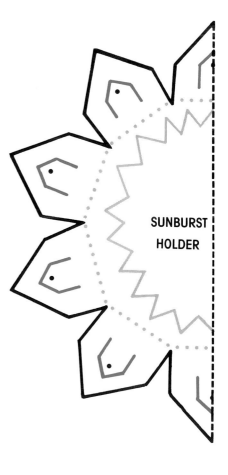

SUNBURST HOLDER

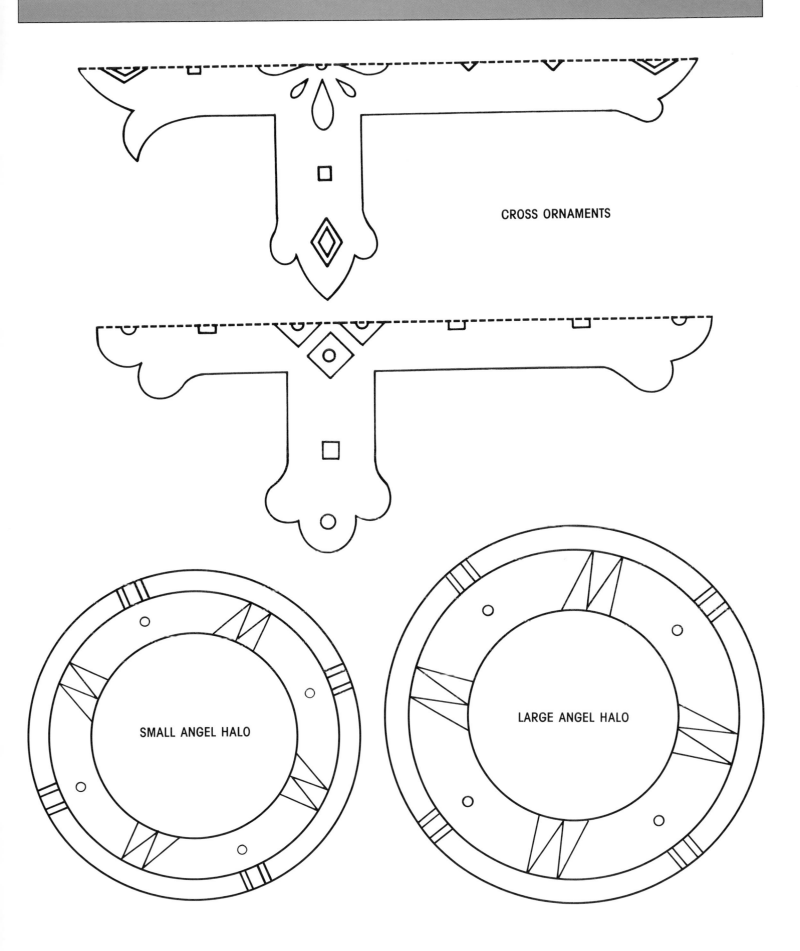

CROSS ORNAMENTS

SMALL ANGEL HALO

LARGE ANGEL HALO

ROMANCING CHRISTMAS

T he beauty of flowers is a rich pleasure, especially in the midst of winter's cold. According to legend, flowers miraculously bloomed the world over on the night Christ was born. From this story came the custom of adorning the Christmas tree with paper roses.

Enchanted by this lovely tradition, we created a collection filled with romantic blossoms and other touches of nature. The flower garden tree is inhabited by sweet bluebirds, each tending its own little nest among bouquets of color-washed paper roses and dried flowers. Grapevines dressed with silk grape leaves encircle the tree, along with garlands of pink and cream pepper berries. Pink German statice is placed among the branches for extra fullness and color, and ribbon streamers add a soft, feminine touch. Rich tapestry fabric is used to create a coordinating tree skirt and stocking.

A filet crochet afghan continues the rose theme, and elements from the tree are repeated in a sentimental bouquet and wreath.

Instructions for the projects shown here and on the next four pages begin on page 66. Experience the romance of roses this Christmas!

As beautiful as an old-fashioned rose garden, the **Romantic Garden Tree** *(page 66)* is filled with touches of nature. Small bouquets of **Paper Roses** *(page 66)* bloom amid a variety of colorful dried flowers, and streamers of wired ribbon wind through the branches. Tucked in willow baskets, tiny bluebirds perch on nests of Spanish moss. Loose grapevines accented with silk grape leaves curve about the tree, along with garlands of pink and cream pepper berries. To further enhance the beauty, sprays of pink German statice nestle among the branches.

A cuff of lacy **Rose Filet Crochet Edging** *(page 69)* gives a feminine air to this richly hued **Romantic Stocking** *(page 68)*. A lovely companion to the tree skirt, it's sure to be filled with sweet remembrances on Christmas morning.

Its distinctive shape a perfect finish for the flower-bedecked tree, our **Octagonal Tree Skirt** *(page 68)* is sewn from rich floral tapestry and edged with upholstery cording. In contrast to the opulence of the skirt, packages are wrapped in simple cream paper and tied with shimmering ribbon.

Holiday celebrations of yore often focused on the ceremonial Yule log. Our version is adorned with **Paper Roses** *(page 66)*, silk grape leaves, burgundy cockscomb, pink German statice, blue and violet peppergrass, pink dudinea, caspia, and a delicate bow.

(Opposite) Bringing classic elegance to any room, the **Rose Filet Crochet Afghan** *(page 69)* offers warmth against the chill of winter. A sentimental bouquet is created by layering elements from the tree — blue and violet peppergrass, caspia, **Paper Roses** *(page 66)*, burgundy cockscomb, pink German statice, and pink dudinea — with sprigs of preserved cedar. The stems are then bound with wired ribbon and accented with silk grape leaves and a ribbon bow.

For a wreath touched with romance, we attached **Paper Roses** *(page 66)*, burgundy cockscomb, preserved cedar, blue ti-tree, and loops of wired ribbon to a purchased caspia wreath.

In **Joyful Christmas** *(page 67)*, a trio of heavenly messengers is gathered to adore the newborn King, who is cradled in a rose-strewn manger. This cross-stitched scene is a lovely way to celebrate the gentle story of Christmas.

65

ROMANTIC GARDEN TREE
(Shown on page 60)

This Romantic Garden tree is a breath of spring at holiday time. The focus of the decorations is on the rose, the most romantic of flowers. Our handmade blossoms look like expensive parchment paper flowers, but are quite easy to make using colored charcoal drawing paper, paint, and a few other supplies. Instructions for making these paper roses are found in this section.

To begin decorating the tree, stems of pink German statice are placed among the branches. A natural garland of dried grapevine which spirals around the tree seems to come to life when silk grape leaves are glued along its length. Artificial pink and cream pepper berry garlands follow the lines of the grapevine, while sprays of darker pepper berries add more color.

The bouquets of flowers look springtime-fresh, but they can be created in midwinter with dried flowers. Small bunches of the paper roses are placed in the tree and then surrounded with a wealth of blossoms. Dried caspia adds a touch of white, while blue and violet peppergrass are airy additions. Burgundy cockscomb balances the lighter colors. Pink and blue dudinea look something like dried hydrangea and provide vibrant color.

The treetop arrangement is simply a larger version of the smaller bouquets. Added to the treetop arrangement and many of the bouquets are streamers of wired ribbon. The ⅞" wide deep pink satin ribbon has wires bound along each edge so that the ribbon may be twisted and formed as desired. Your local craft store or florist can help you find the ribbon and dried materials or suggest suitable substitutes.

Every garden needs birds, and this garden tree is complete when bluebirds are added. Three-inch oval willow baskets filled with Spanish moss serve as nests when hung from branches. The tiny white-breasted birds are perched on the edges of the baskets or nestled in their mossy nests.

The elegant tree skirt fashioned from tapestry upholstery fabric is made in a striking octagonal shape. A decorative twisted cording is added to its edges. This tree skirt is the perfect finish for the lovely decorations on this Romantic Garden tree.

PAPER ROSES (Shown on page 62)

For each rose, you will need green and pink or cream 64 lb. charcoal drawing paper; 18-gauge florist wire; brown crepe florist tape; craft glue; wire cutters; green, pink, and mauve acrylic paint; small round paintbrushes; spring-type clothespins; spray bottle filled with water; craft knife; tracing paper; and lightweight cardboard.

1. Trace petal and leaf patterns onto tracing paper and cut out. For petal and leaf templates, use patterns and cut one petal piece and one leaf piece from cardboard. For rose center template, cut one 1½" x 5" piece from cardboard.
2. Using pencil and leaf template, draw around desired number of leaves on green paper. Using petal and rose center templates, draw around two petals and one rose center on pink or cream paper. Tear out pieces along pencil lines. Erase any remaining pencil marks. Thoroughly crumple all paper pieces; unfold pieces and lay flat. Use craft knife to cut a small **x** through each petal piece where indicated on pattern.
3. For stem, cut desired length of florist wire. Bend one end ½" to one side to form a loop.
4. For rose center, apply a line of glue along one long edge of rose center piece. Beginning at one short edge and pinching glued area around wire, loosely wrap piece around looped end of wire to within 1" of remaining short edge (**Fig. 1**). Use clothespin to hold wrapped area in place until glue is almost dry. Remove clothespin.

Fig. 1

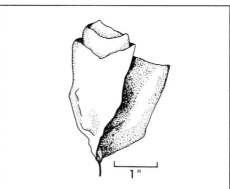

5. For first petal piece, apply glue around cut area at center of one petal piece. Insert end of florist wire through center of petal piece, pushing glued area of petal piece snugly against

bottom of rose center. Tightly pinch glued area of piece around rose center and wire. Use clothespin to hold glued area in place until glue is almost dry. Remove clothespin. Repeat for remaining petal piece.
6. To paint rose and leaves, dilute each color of paint to a very watery consistency. Spray rose generously with water. Allowing paint to run, brush pink paint along edges of each petal, sides of rose center, and undersides of petals. While still wet, brush mauve paint along edges of petals only. Spray leaves generously with water. Allowing paint to run, brush green paint along edges and center of each leaf. Allow to dry.
7. To attach leaves, wrap top of rose stem with florist tape; at desired intervals, tape leaves to stem. Wrap remainder of stem with florist tape.

JOYFUL CHRISTMAS (83w x 119h)

X	DMC	¼X	½X	B'ST	ANC.	COLOR
⬚	blanc	⬚			02	white
⬛	347			╱	013	dk rose
A	353	◣			08	peach
⬛	433		▨		0358	lt brown
⬛	434			╱	0371	dk tan
✳	436				0369	tan
★	500				0879	dk green
E	501				0877	green
▢	503				0875	lt green
⊙	645				0400	grey
−	676	◣			0891	lt gold
O	712				0387	cream
8	738				0367	lt tan
+	739				0366	vy lt tan
N	754	◣			4146	lt peach
⊙	758	◣			9575	dk peach
2	760				010	lt rose
X	761	◣			09	vy lt rose
☆	783				0307	gold
⬛	801				0359	brown
	838	◣	▨	╱	0380	dk brown
▨	951				0880	vy lt peach
S	3023				8581	beige grey
S	3033				0900	lt beige grey
△	3328			╱	011	rose

JOYFUL CHRISTMAS (83w x 119h)	
Aida 11	7⅝" x 10⅞"
Aida 14	6" x 8½"
Aida 18	4⅝" x 6⅝"
Hardanger 22	3⅞" x 5½"

JOYFUL CHRISTMAS (Shown on page 65)

You will need one 12" x 15" piece of Tea-Dyed Irish Linen (28 ct), embroidery floss (see color key, page 66), embroidery hoop (optional), and frame.

1. Work design over 2 fabric threads. Use 2 strands of floss for Cross Stitch, 1 for Half Cross Stitch, and 1 for Backstitch.

2. Frame as desired (we used a custom frame).

OCTAGONAL TREE SKIRT (Shown on page 63)

You will need one 54" square of fabric for tree skirt (we used upholstery fabric), one 54" square of fabric for lining (pieced as necessary), 4⅛ yds of decorative upholstery cording, thread to match fabric, thumbtack or pin, fabric marking pencil, and string.

1. Fold lining fabric in half from top to bottom and again from left to right. Referring to **Fig. 1**, match folded edges and fold in half again.

Fig. 1

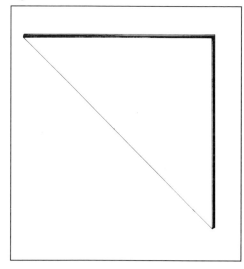

2. To mark outer cutting line, refer to **Fig. 2** and use fabric marking pencil to draw a straight line between folded edges 24" from center.

Fig. 2

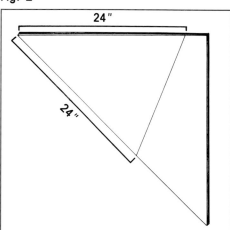

3. To mark inner cutting line, tie one end of string to fabric marking pencil. Insert thumbtack through string 2" from pencil. Insert thumbtack in fabric as shown in **Fig. 3** and mark one-eighth of a circle.

Fig. 3

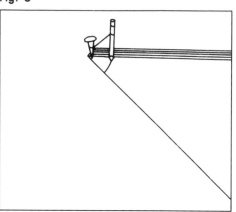

4. Following cutting lines and cutting through all thicknesses of fabric, cut out lining piece. For opening in back of skirt, cut along one fold from outer to inner edge.

5. Place lining and tree skirt fabric right sides together. Use lining as a pattern and cut tree skirt from fabric.

6. Fold one end of cording ½" to one side and whipstitch in place. Referring to **Fig. 4**, begin basting cording to outer edge of tree skirt fabric ½" from one edge of skirt opening. Clipping cording at corners, continue basting cording to edge of skirt to within ½" of remaining edge of skirt opening. Cut cording even with edge of skirt opening. Fold end of cording ½" to one side and whipstitch in place.

Fig. 4

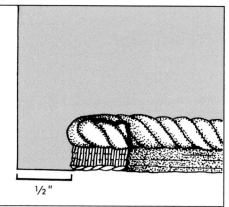

7. (**Note:** Use a ½" seam allowance.) With right sides together and leaving an opening for turning, use zipper foot and sew tree skirt fabric and lining together; clip curves and cut corners diagonally. Turn tree skirt right side out and press; sew final closure by hand.

ROMANTIC STOCKING
(Shown on page 62)

You will need two 12" x 18" pieces of fabric for stocking (we used upholstery fabric), two 12" x 18" pieces of fabric for lining, one 16½" x 4¾" piece of fabric for cuff, thread to match fabrics, tracing paper, fabric marking pencil, 16" of Rose Filet Crochet Edging (page 69), and 5" of ⅜" wide satin ribbon.

1. Matching arrows to form one pattern, trace outline of stocking pattern, pages 16 and 17, onto tracing paper; cut out pattern.
2. Leaving top edge open, use pattern and stocking fabric pieces and follow **Sewing Shapes**, page 156, to make stocking.
3. With right sides together and matching short edges, fold cuff piece in half. Use a ¼" seam allowance to sew short edges together. Press seam open.
4. Press one long edge (bottom) of cuff ½" to wrong side and hem.
5. Beginning at cuff seamline, match long straight edge of crochet edging to top edge of right side of cuff. Baste edging to cuff along straight edge, easing to fit if necessary. Tack short edges of edging together.
6. With wrong side of cuff facing right side of stocking, and matching top edges, pin cuff to stocking. Use a ½" seam allowance and sew pieces together. Press top edge of stocking ½" to wrong side.
7. For lining, use lining fabric pieces and repeat Step 2; do not turn right side out. Press top edge of lining ¾" to wrong side. With wrong sides facing, insert lining into stocking; pin pieces together.
8. For hanger, fold ribbon in half, matching ends. Place ends of ribbon between lining and stocking at right seamline with approximately 2" of hanger extending above stocking; pin in place.
9. Slipstitch lining to stocking and, at the same time, securely sew hanger in place.

ROSE FILET CROCHET (Shown on pages 62 and 64)

ABBREVIATIONS
ch(s)   chain(s)
dc   double crochet(s)
sl st   slip stitch
st(s)   stitch(es)
YO   yarn over

( ) or [ ] — work enclosed instructions **as many** times as specified by the number immediately following **or** contains explanatory remarks.

WORKING WITH CHARTS
Each blank square on the chart represents one Space (ch 2, dc) and each grey square represents one Block (3 dc). For right side rows, the chart should be read from right to left; for wrong side rows, the chart should be read from left to right.

EDGING

Finished Size: Approximately 4½" wide

MATERIALS
DMC Cebelia Art. 167/size 30, ecru — one ball (approximately 563 yards)
Steel crochet hook, size 10 (1.15 mm) **or** size needed for gauge

GAUGE: 18 dc and 6 rows = 1"
   DO NOT HESITATE TO CHANGE HOOK SIZE TO OBTAIN CORRECT GAUGE.

INSTRUCTIONS
Ch 69 **loosely**.
Row 1 (Right side): Dc in 4th ch from hook and in next 2 chs, ch 2, skip 2 chs, dc in next 4 chs, (ch 2, skip 2 chs, dc in next ch) 14 times, dc in next 3 chs, (ch 2, skip 2 chs, dc in next ch) 2 times, dc in last 6 chs.
Row 2: (Ch 3, turn, dc in next 3 dc **(beginning Block over Block made)**), (dc in next 3 dc **(Block over Block made)**), (ch 2, dc in next dc **(Space over Space made)**), (work 2 dc in next Space, dc in next dc **(Block over Space made)**), (ch 2, skip 2 dc, dc in next dc **(Space over Block made)**), follow chart across, work end increase as follows: (YO, insert hook into base of last dc and pull up a loop, YO and draw through one loop on hook, (YO and draw through 2 loops on hook) twice) 3 times.
Row 3: (Ch 5, turn, dc in 4th ch from

hook and in next ch, dc in next dc **(beginning increase made)**), follow chart across.
Rows 4-6: Follow chart.
Row 7: (Turn, sl st in first 4 dc, ch 3 **(beginning decrease made)**), follow chart across.
Row 8: Follow chart across, leaving last 3 sts unworked.
Rows 9-22: Follow chart.
Repeat Rows 1-22 until edging is desired length; finish off.

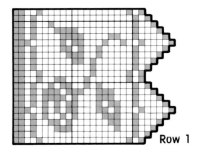
Row 1

AFGHAN

Finished Size: Approximately 46" x 73"

MATERIALS
100% Cotton Worsted Weight Yarn, approximately: 57½ ounces (1631 grams, 2934 yds)
Crochet hook, size F (4.00 mm) **or** size needed for gauge

GAUGE: 16 dc and 8 rows = 4"
   DO NOT HESITATE TO CHANGE HOOK SIZE TO OBTAIN CORRECT GAUGE.

INSTRUCTIONS
Ch 258 **loosely**.
Row 1 (Right side): Dc in 4th ch from hook and in next 254 chs.
Row 2: (Ch 5, turn, dc in 4th ch from hook and in next ch, dc in next dc **(beginning increase made)**), (ch 2, skip 2 dc, dc in next dc **(Space over Block made)**), (dc in next 3 dc **(Block over Block made)**), follow chart across, work end increase as follows: (YO, insert hook into base of last dc and pull up a loop, YO and draw through one loop on hook, (YO and draw through 2 loops on hook) twice) 3 times.

Row 3: Work beginning increase, work Space, (work 2 dc in next Space, dc in next dc **(Block over Space made)**), work Space, (ch 2, dc in next dc **(Space over Space made)**) 16 times, follow chart across.
Rows 4-7: Follow chart.
Row 8: (Turn, sl st in first 4 dc, ch 3 **(beginning decrease made)**), follow chart across, leaving last 3 sts unworked.
Rows 9-12: Follow chart.
Row 13: (Ch 3, turn, dc in next 3 dc **(beginning Block over Block made)**), follow chart across.
Rows 14-24: Follow chart.
Rows 25-93: Following chart, repeat Rows 2-24, 3 times; finish off.

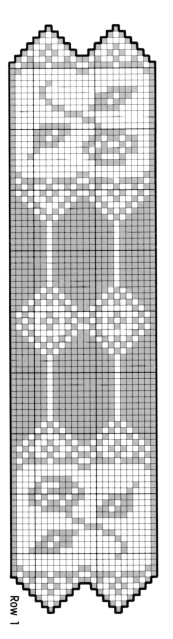
Row 1

COUNTRY HOLIDAY

Down on the farm, Christmas is a cheerful occasion, celebrated with handcrafted decorations that reflect the simple charm of life in the country.

This lighthearted collection brings to mind images of cows grazing peacefully, hens clucking contentedly, and farmhouses surrounded by neat picket fences. A star-shaped Santa, clad in farmer's overalls, tops the tree, while a host of animal angels keeps watch over the farm's residents. In honor of the friendly cow, spotted ornaments and miniature copper cowbells with calico bows adorn the branches. Accented by paper picket fences, speckled hens nest in little market baskets, and tiny tin pails of cranberries lend colorful highlights. Tin icicles and raffia bows trimmed with hearts add homey touches. And blackbirds perch on a wooden fence around the tree, perhaps hoping to snatch a stray berry for their dinner.

Above the fireplace, a grapevine wreath sports another Santa star, and a pair of country stockings awaits a visit from Santa Bunny.

Instructions for the projects shown here and on the next six pages begin on page 78. Enjoy a country holiday!

A clever pair of **Speckled Hen Ornaments** *(page 78)* has taken up residence in a tin grain scoop. We made their nest from hay and peppergrass and tied a calico bow to the handle.

Opening gifts on Christmas morning is sure to be a "moo-ving" experience with this whimsical wrapping paper! To make it, draw spots on cream wrapping paper; then fill in the spots with black acrylic paint. Jute bows and miniature copper cowbells provide cute trimmings. For delightful country accents, painted grosgrain ribbon adorns tin milk cans, and a tin colander is filled with **Spotted Cow Ornaments** *(page 79)*.

A shiny copper bell announces holiday visitors with a merry jingle. To make this simple door decoration, just attach a cowbell to a loop of braided jute and add a big bow of torn gingham fabric.

The **Country Holiday Tree** *(page 78)* has farm-fresh charm. Lovable bunnies, bears, dogs, cats, and sheep dressed as **Animal Angels** *(page 80)* are surrounded by sections of a **Farm Fence Garland** *(page 78)*. **Speckled Hen Ornaments** *(page 78)* nestled in little market baskets share the tree with **Spotted Cow Ornaments** *(page 79)*. Tiny tin pails of cranberries are hung here and there, along with miniature cowbells tied with calico bows. Shiny **Tin Icicles** *(page 78)* glimmer among the branches, and natural raffia bows are accented with painted wooden hearts.

Santa's sure to fill these fleece-trimmed **Country Stockings** *(page 79)* with lots of goodies! There's one of rugged plaid for the man of the house and a red one with a sweet **Animal Angel** *(page 80)* for the lady.

This lighthearted wreath is a fun way to deck the halls with holiday cheer. Poised in a grapevine wreath, a **Santa Star** *(page 81)* sports denim overalls and a plaid shirt and cap. At his feet, a **Speckled Hen Ornament** *(page 78)* has made a cozy nest of peppergrass, hay, excelsior, wheat stalks, and sprigs of evergreen.

A mailbox overflowing with hay, peppergrass, and wheat stalks has attracted some inquisitive blackbirds. What a cute place to display Christmas cards!

When friends drop by to exchange holiday greetings, surprise them with tiny goody baskets filled with candy or snack crackers. We trimmed little market baskets with country fabrics and lined them with excelsior to hold our treats.

To create a country accent that will brighten any spot, attach several **Animal Angels** *(page 80)* to a jute ''clothesline'' with wooden clothespins.

It's easy to imagine this adorable choir of standing **Animal Angels** *(page 80)* caroling for their barnyard friends on a frosty winter night. A red and cream **Shoofly Quilt Wall Hanging** *(page 79)* provides a festive backdrop.

With long floppy ears and oversized feet, **Santa Bunny** *(page 83)* looks like an old-fashioned toy. To prepare him for his special role on Christmas Eve, we dressed our little friend in a red suit trimmed with fleece. To wrap the packages he'll soon deliver, we sprayed sheets of newspaper with glossy wood tone spray and tied the packages with gingham ribbon.

COUNTRY HOLIDAY TREE
(Shown on page 70)

Welcome the spirit and warmth of all things country into your home for the holiday season. Topped off with a star-shaped Santa decked out in overalls, this Christmas tree is full of easy country crafts. Instructions can be found in this section for the paper farm fence garland, tin icicles, "spotted cow" glass ball ornaments, angelic animals in homespun dresses, and stuffed and painted hen ornaments.

The speckled hen ornaments are nestled in purchased 3" long market baskets filled with excelsior and trimmed with strips of gingham. Other purchased items include 2¼" high tin pails filled with festive, fresh cranberries and 1" high brass cowbells tied to the branches with strips of fabric. Raffia bows with long, wispy streamers have painted wooden hearts glued at the centers.

To complete this Country Holiday scene, an 18" high white picket fence purchased at a garden center stands around the base of the tree. Perched on the fence are artificial birds spray-painted black to resemble crows.

TIN ICICLES
(Shown on page 73)

For each icicle, you will need one ¼" x 4½" strip of aluminum flashing (available at hardware stores), utility scissors, hammer, small nail, and 4" of nylon line (for hanger).

1. (**Note:** Cut edges of flashing may be sharp.) Refer to **Fig. 1** to twist flashing strip.

Fig. 1

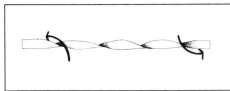

2. Use scissors to cut one end of strip diagonally.
3. Use hammer and nail to make a hole ½" from remaining end of strip. Thread nylon line through hole and knot ends of line together.

FARM FENCE GARLAND   (Shown on page 73)

For each garland, you will need one 3½" x 25" strip of natural parchment paper; small, sharp scissors; tracing paper; graphite transfer paper; and removable tape.

1. Fold one short end of parchment paper 2½" to one side. Using fold as a guide, fanfold remaining length of paper. Use tape to hold edges of paper together so paper will not shift when cutting.
2. Trace farm fence pattern onto tracing paper. With dashed lines of pattern on folds and bottom edge of pattern even with one short edge of paper, use transfer paper to transfer pattern to folded paper.
3. Cutting on solid lines only, cut out garland.

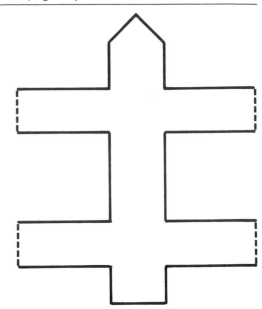

SPECKLED HEN ORNAMENTS   (Shown on pages 72 and 73)

For each ornament, you will need two 5" squares of unbleached muslin fabric; thread to match fabric; tracing paper; fabric marking pencil; small crochet hook (to turn fabric); polyester fiberfill; red, yellow, and black acrylic paint; small round paintbrush; and plastic fork.

1. Using hen pattern and fabric squares, follow **Transferring Patterns** and **Sewing Shapes**, page 156, to make hen. Stuff hen with fiberfill; sew final closure by hand.
2. Referring to photo and pattern, paint comb red, beak yellow, and eyes black. For feathers, use fork dipped in black paint to paint dots. Allow to dry.

SHOOFLY QUILT WALL HANGING (Shown on page 76)

For a 35¾" x 24¾" wall hanging, you will need 1 yd of red 44"w cotton fabric, ½ yd of 38"w unbleached muslin fabric, ½ yd of 44"w cotton fabric for bias binding, 1 yd of 44"w cotton fabric for backing and hanging sleeve, one 28" x 39" piece of low-loft polyester bonded batting, one 5" x 8" piece of acetate, fabric marking pencil, thread to match fabric, yellow embroidery floss, and one 35" length of ½" dia. wooden dowel.

Note: For each sewing step, pin fabric pieces right sides together, matching raw edges. Use a ¼" seam allowance throughout. Press seam allowances to one side.

1. Wash, dry, and press all fabrics. Trim selvages from fabrics.
2. For square template, cut one 3½" square from acetate. For triangle template, cut one 3⅞" square from acetate; cut square in half diagonally and use one-half of square for template.
3. Use templates to cut 6 squares and 24 triangles from red fabric; cut 24 squares and 24 triangles from muslin fabric.
4. Sew one red and one muslin triangle together along long edges. Repeat with remaining triangles to make 24 pieced squares.

5. For each block, refer to Diagram and sew pieced and solid squares together.
6. For sashing and borders, cut three 2½" x 9½" pieces, four 2½" x 20½" pieces, and two 2½" x 35½" pieces from red fabric.
7. To assemble quilt top, refer to Diagram to sew blocks, sashing, and borders together.
8. Cut backing fabric and batting 1" larger on all sides than quilt top. Place batting on wrong side of backing. Center quilt top, right side up, on batting. Baste layers together from corner to corner and from side to side.
9. To tie quilt, thread needle with a 5" length of floss. Referring to photo, go down through all layers at one tie position and come up ⅛" away. Securely knot floss close to fabric; trim ends to ¾". Repeat for each tie.

10. Trim batting and backing even with quilt top.
11. For hanging sleeve, cut a 6" x 35" piece from sleeve fabric. Press short edges of fabric piece ¼" to wrong side; press ¼" to wrong side again. Stitch close to folded edges. With wrong sides together, fold fabric in half lengthwise and press. Matching raw edges, center hanging sleeve at top back of quilt. Baste raw edges together. Whipstitch fold of sleeve to backing.
12. For binding, cut one 1½" x 124" bias strip from binding fabric (pieced as necessary). Matching wrong sides and raw edges, fold bias strip in half lengthwise; press. Press long raw edges to center. Apply binding to edge of quilt. Remove basting threads. Insert dowel in hanging sleeve.

DIAGRAM

COUNTRY STOCKINGS (Shown on page 74)

For each stocking, you will need two 12" x 18" pieces and one 1½" x 8" piece of fabric for stocking and hanger, two 12" x 18" pieces of fabric for lining, one 4" x 16½" piece of artificial lamb fleece for cuff, thread to match fabric and fleece, tracing paper, and fabric marking pencil.
For each animal angel stocking, you will also need desired Animal Angel with star (page 80).

1. Matching arrows to form one pattern, trace outline of stocking pattern, pages 16 and 17, onto tracing paper; cut out.
2. Leaving top edge open, use pattern and follow **Sewing Shapes**, page 156, to make stocking from stocking fabric pieces. Do not turn right side out.
3. For cuff, match right sides and short edges and fold fleece in half. Using a ½" seam allowance, sew short edges together to form a tube. Fold one raw

edge ½" to wrong side; whipstitch in place.
4. To attach cuff to stocking, place cuff over stocking with right side of cuff facing wrong side of stocking and matching raw edges. Using a ½" seam allowance, sew raw edges together. Trim seam allowance and turn stocking right side out. Fold cuff down over stocking.
5. For lining, use lining fabric pieces and repeat Step 2. Press top edge of lining ½" to wrong side.
6. With wrong sides together, insert lining into stocking and pin in place.
7. For hanger, press long edges of 1½" x 8" fabric piece ¼" to wrong side. With wrong sides together, fold hanger piece in half lengthwise; sew close to folded edges. Matching ends, fold hanger in half to form a loop. Place ends of hanger between lining and

stocking at right seamline with approximately 3" of loop extending above stocking; pin in place.
8. Slipstitch lining to stocking and, at the same time, securely sew hanger in place.
9. For animal angel stocking, refer to photo and tack angel to stocking.

SPOTTED COW ORNAMENTS (Shown on page 73)

You will need desired size glass ball ornaments, matte ivory spray paint, paintbrush, and black acrylic paint.

1. Spray ornaments with a light coat of ivory paint; allow to dry. Repeat until ornaments are evenly coated with paint.
2. Referring to photo, use a pencil to draw spots on ornaments. Paint spots black; allow to dry.

ANIMAL ANGELS (Shown on pages 73 and 76)

For each angel, you will need one 12" x 16" piece of unbleached muslin fabric for body, two 6" x 8" pieces of unbleached muslin fabric for wings, two 9" x 11" pieces of fabric for dress, one 6" x 8" piece of craft batting, thread to match fabrics, polyester fiberfill, small crochet hook (to turn fabric), heavy thread (buttonhole twist) to match muslin, ecru embroidery floss, black permanent felt-tip pen with fine point, black colored pencil, matte clear acrylic spray, instant coffee, fabric marking pencil, tracing paper, and bird gravel (for standing angel only).

For each star, you will also need two 5" squares of fabric and thread to match fabric.

1. Dissolve 1 tablespoon of instant coffee in 1 cup of hot water; allow to cool. Soak muslin for body in coffee for several minutes. Remove from coffee and allow to dry; press.

2. Use body, arm, and desired ear patterns, on this page and page 81, and follow **Transferring Patterns**, page 156. For each shape, cut two pieces of coffee-dyed muslin 1" larger than pattern on all sides. Follow **Sewing Shapes**, page 156, to make one body, two arms, and two ears.

3. (**Note:** For standing angel only, use bird gravel to stuff lower one-fourth of body.) Stuff body with fiberfill to within 1" of opening. Fold fabric over opening as shown in **Fig. 1**; whipstitch in place.

Fig. 1

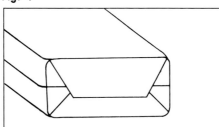

4. Press raw edges of ears ⅛" to wrong side. Refer to photo to position ears on body at seamline; whipstitch in place.

5. Stuff lower one-third of each arm with fiberfill. Press raw edge of each arm ⅛" to wrong side. Refer to **Fig. 2** to position arms on body at seamline; whipstitch in place.

Fig. 2

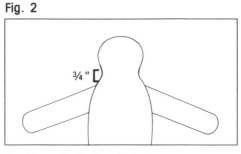

6. (**Note:** Refer to photo for Steps 6 — 8.) For bear, cat, or rabbit, use pen to draw facial features.

7. For cat or rabbit whiskers, thread needle with three 6" lengths of heavy thread. Run needle through face; unthread needle. Knot lengths together at each side of face and trim ends to ½".

8. For sheep or dog, color face and ears with black pencil. Lightly spray face and ears with acrylic spray; allow to dry. Use pen to draw facial features of dog. For sheep eyes, use 6 strands of floss and work French Knots.

9. For dress, use dress pattern, page 81, and follow **Transferring Patterns**, page 156. Sewing sleeve and side seams only, follow **Sewing Shapes**, page 156. Cut sleeves, neck, and bottom of dress on pencil lines.

10. Press neck and sleeve edges ¼" to wrong side. Baste close to folded edges. Place dress on angel and pull basting threads to gather fabric around neck and arms; knot threads and trim ends. Fringe bottom edge of dress ⅛".

11. For wings, use wings pattern, page 81, and follow **Transferring Patterns**, page 156. Place batting piece on flat surface and center remaining muslin pieces on top. Follow **Sewing Shapes**, page 156, trimming batting as close as possible to seam. Sew final closure by hand. Refer to photo and tack wings to back of dress.

12. For star, use star pattern, page 81, and follow **Transferring Patterns** and **Sewing Shapes**, page 156, to make star from star fabric. Stuff star with fiberfill and sew final closure by hand. Tack star to angel.

BODY

Leave Open

ARM

Leave Open

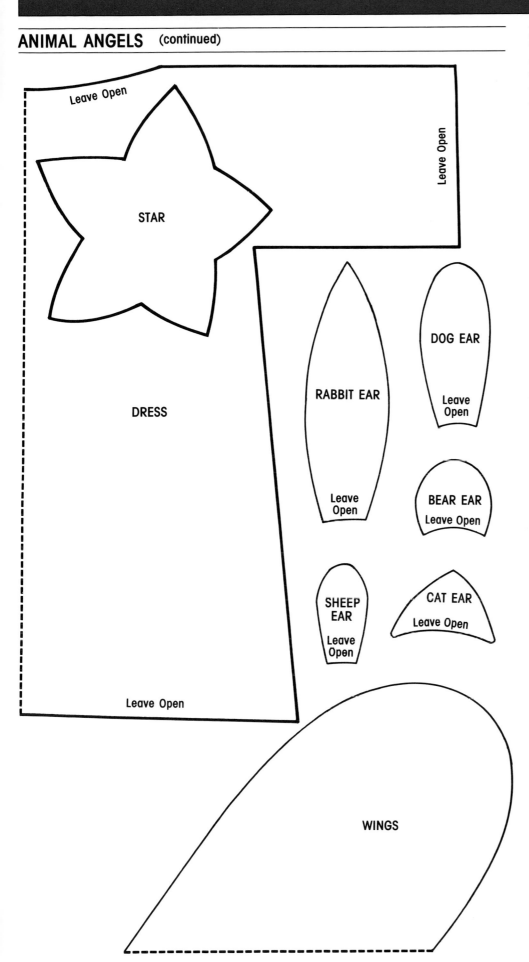

STAR

DRESS

Leave Open

Leave Open

Leave Open

RABBIT EAR

Leave Open

DOG EAR

Leave Open

BEAR EAR

Leave Open

SHEEP EAR

Leave Open

CAT EAR

Leave Open

WINGS

SANTA STAR

(Shown on pages 70 and 74)

You will need ½ yd of 44"w plaid fabric for star and hat, one 7" x 9" piece of denim for overalls and straps, one 4" x 9½" piece of artificial lamb fleece for trim, one 2½" x 5" piece of black felt for boots, one 2½" x 4" piece of unbleached muslin for face, 1 yd of wool roving for beard, pink colored pencil, one ³⁄₁₆" dia. red button for nose, tan thread and thread to match plaid fabric and wool roving, craft glue, black embroidery floss, ecru heavy thread (buttonhole twist), polyester fiberfill, tracing paper, paper-backed fusible web, lightweight fusible interfacing, hot glue gun, glue sticks, fabric marking pencil, transparent tape, and one 7" long pitchfork (optional).

1. Use Santa star top and Santa star bottom patterns, page 82, and follow **Transferring Patterns**, page 156. Matching arrows to form one pattern, tape patterns together. Use pattern and trace separate overalls, strap, face, and boot patterns onto tracing paper and cut out.
2. Cut interfacing and web slightly smaller than overalls, face, and boot fabric pieces. Follow manufacturer's instructions to fuse interfacing and web to wrong sides of fabric pieces.
3. Use patterns and cut two stars, one face, one overalls, two straps (cut one in reverse), and two boots from fabrics.
4. Referring to pattern for placement, fuse overalls, straps, face, and boots to right side of one star piece.
5. Refer to dotted lines on pattern and use tan thread to topstitch around overalls and boots.
6. (**Note:** Refer to photo for Steps 6 − 8.) For eyes, refer to pattern and use 6 strands of floss to work French Knots.
7. Use pink pencil to lightly color cheeks.
8. For nose, sew button to face.
9. With right sides facing and leaving an opening for turning, use a ¼" seam allowance and sew star pieces together. Cut outside corners diagonally and clip inside corners close to seam; turn star right side out.
10. Stuff star firmly with fiberfill. Sew final closure by hand.

Continued on page 82

SANTA STAR (continued)

11. For trim on arms, cut two ½" x 4½" pieces from fleece. Refer to photo and glue strips to arms.

12. For beard, divide wool roving in half lengthwise. Refer to **Fig. 1** to arrange roving, gently shaping roving until beard measures approximately 7" wide. Tack top folds of beard together. Use craft glue to secure top of beard to face.

Fig. 1

13. For boot laces, thread needle with heavy thread and refer to photo to make stitches resembling laces. Tie ends of thread in a bow and trim ends.

14. For hat, follow Steps 1 — 4 of Santa Bunny Clothing instructions, page 83, omitting jingle bell and openings for ears. Fold raw edge of hat trim ½" to wrong side; whipstitch in place.

15. Place hat on head and hot glue pitchfork to hand.

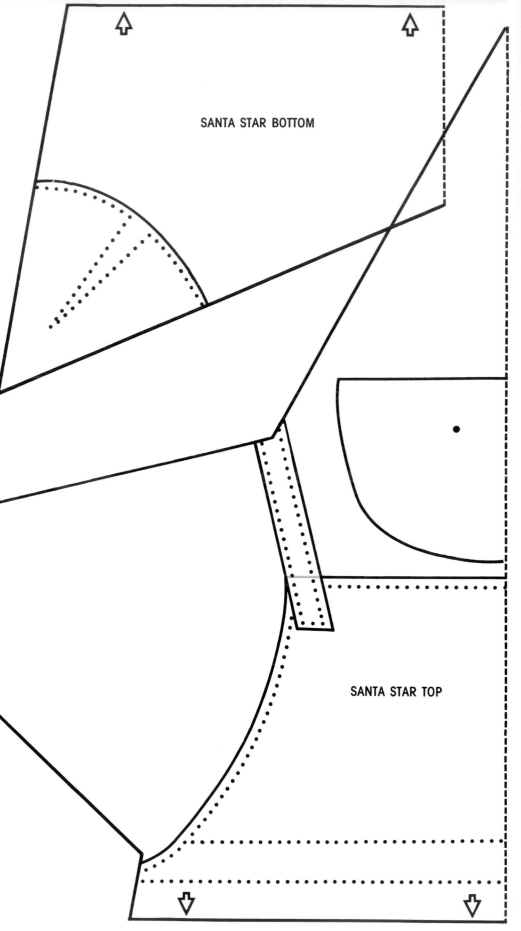

SANTA STAR BOTTOM

SANTA STAR TOP

SANTA BUNNY (Shown on page 77)

For bunny, you will need ½ yd of 38"w unbleached muslin, two ⅜" dia. blue buttons for eyes, thread to match muslin, ecru heavy thread (buttonhole twist), soft sculpture needle, polyester fiberfill, tan embroidery floss, tracing paper, fabric marking pencil, small crochet hook (to turn fabric), and instant coffee.

For clothing, you will also need one 17" x 18" piece of fabric for shirt, ⅜ yd of 44"w fabric for trousers and suspenders, one 29" x 18" piece of fabric for coat and hat, two 3" x 8" pieces of fabric for collar, five ½" dia. buttons for coat, two ⅜" dia. buttons for shirt, one 18" x 14" piece of artificial lamb fleece for coat and hat trim, one 15mm jingle bell, string, thumbtack or pin, seam ripper, and thread to match fabrics.

Note: Use a ¼" seam allowance throughout. Clip curves and cut corners diagonally.

BUNNY

1. Use body, arm, leg, and ear patterns, pages 84 and 85, and follow Steps 1 and 2 of Animal Angel instructions, page 80, to make one body, two arms, two legs, and two ears.
2. Stuff body, arms, and legs with fiberfill. Sew final closures of all shapes by hand.
3. For tuck at base of each ear, refer to pattern and fold ear along solid grey line. Match fold to dotted grey line; baste in place.
4. Referring to body pattern, match short edges of ears to placement lines on body; whipstitch ears to body. Remove basting threads.
5. Thread soft sculpture needle with a strand of heavy thread; knot ends of thread together. For eyes, refer to photo and pattern and insert needle through body at one ●. Thread needle through one blue button and insert needle back through body. Thread needle through remaining blue button and insert needle back through body. Repeat to make several more stitches through buttons and body, pulling tightly to indent eyes.
6. For arms and legs, refer to **Fig. 1** and repeat Step 5 to attach arms at ■'s and legs at ♦'s.

Fig. 1

7. Referring to photo and **Embroidery Stitch Diagrams**, page 158, use 6 strands of floss and Satin Stitch to work nose; use Straight Stitch to work mouth.
8. For whiskers, thread needle with two 4½" lengths of heavy thread. Referring to photo, run needle through face; unthread needle. Knot lengths together on each side of face. Repeat for remaining set of whiskers.

CLOTHING

1. For hat pattern, cut a 15" square of tracing paper; fold in half diagonally and cut along fold line. Discard one half. Tie one end of string to fabric marking pencil. Insert thumbtack through string 13" from pencil. Insert thumbtack in one corner of paper as shown in **Fig. 2** and mark cutting line; cut out.

Fig. 2

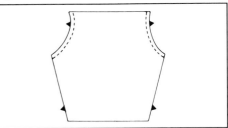

2. Use pattern and cut one hat piece from fabric. With right sides facing and matching straight edges, fold hat piece in half; sew straight edges together. Turn hat right side out.
3. For hat trim, cut a 2" x 10¼" piece of fleece. Matching right sides and short edges, fold fleece in half; sew short edges together.
4. With right sides together, match seams and one raw edge of hat trim to one raw edge of hat; sew hat trim to hat. For openings for bunny ears, use

seam ripper to open seam on each side of hat, 1" from center back seam. Sew bell to point of hat. Set hat aside.
5. Use trousers, shirt, coat, and pocket patterns, page 85, and follow **Transferring Patterns**, page 156. Use patterns and cut pieces from fabrics.
6. For trousers, match right sides and notches of fabric pieces and sew center seams (**Fig. 3**).

Fig. 3

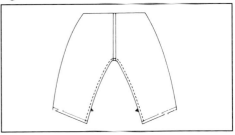

7. Press bottom raw edges of trousers ¼" to wrong side; stitch in place.
8. With right sides together and matching center seams, sew trouser leg seam (**Fig. 4**). Turn trousers right side out.

Fig. 4

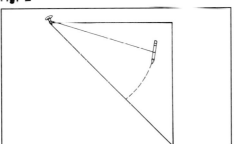

9. For each pleat at top of trousers, refer to pattern and fold fabric along solid grey line. Match fold to dotted grey line; baste in place.
10. Press top raw edge of trousers ½" to wrong side; stitch ¼" from pressed edge.
11. For suspenders, cut two 2½" x 10" pieces from fabric. With right sides facing, fold one piece of fabric in half lengthwise; sew long edges together. Trim seam allowance to ⅛". Turn suspender right side out; press. Topstitch ⅛" from each long edge. Repeat for remaining suspender.
12. Referring to photo, place ½" of one end of each suspender inside front of trousers; stitch in place. Set trousers aside.

Continued on page 84

SANTA BUNNY (continued)

13. For shirt, match right sides and raw edges and sew pieces together along top of arms from outer edges to ♦'s; sew along sides and under arms. For front opening, cut along center of one shirt piece.

14. Press neck, bottom, and shirt opening edges ¼" to wrong side; stitch in place.

15. Press raw edge of each sleeve ½" to wrong side; baste pressed edge in place.

16. Refer to photo and sew buttons on left side of shirt opening.

17. Place shirt on bunny, overlapping edges; tack shirt opening closed. Pull basting threads on each sleeve, gathering sleeve to fit around wrist of bunny. Knot thread and trim ends.

18. For collar, use collar pattern, page 85, and fabric and follow **Transferring Patterns** and **Sewing Shapes**, page 156. Press collar and sew final closure by hand. Refer to photo to place collar around neck of bunny; tack in place.

19. For coat, follow Step 13 of Clothing instructions. Press each edge of coat opening ¼" to wrong side; stitch in place.

20. For pockets, press raw edges on each pocket piece ¼" to wrong side. With bottom of pocket ¾" from bottom edge of coat and one side of pocket ¾" from opening, stitch bottom and side edges of one pocket to each side of coat.

21. Refer to photo and sew buttons to coat along right side of coat opening.

22. For fleece trim, cut two 2" x 8½" pieces for sleeves, one 1½" x 9" piece for neck, and one 2" x 16½" piece for bottom trim.

23. For each trim, fold short edges and one long edge ¼" to wrong side; whipstitch in place.

24. With right sides together and matching raw edges, sew trims to coat. For sleeve trim, whipstitch short edges together.

25. Place trousers on bunny. Place suspenders over shoulders, cross suspenders in back, and tack remaining ends inside back of trousers. Place coat on bunny. Place hat on bunny, inserting ears through openings.

BODY

ear placement

EAR

LEG

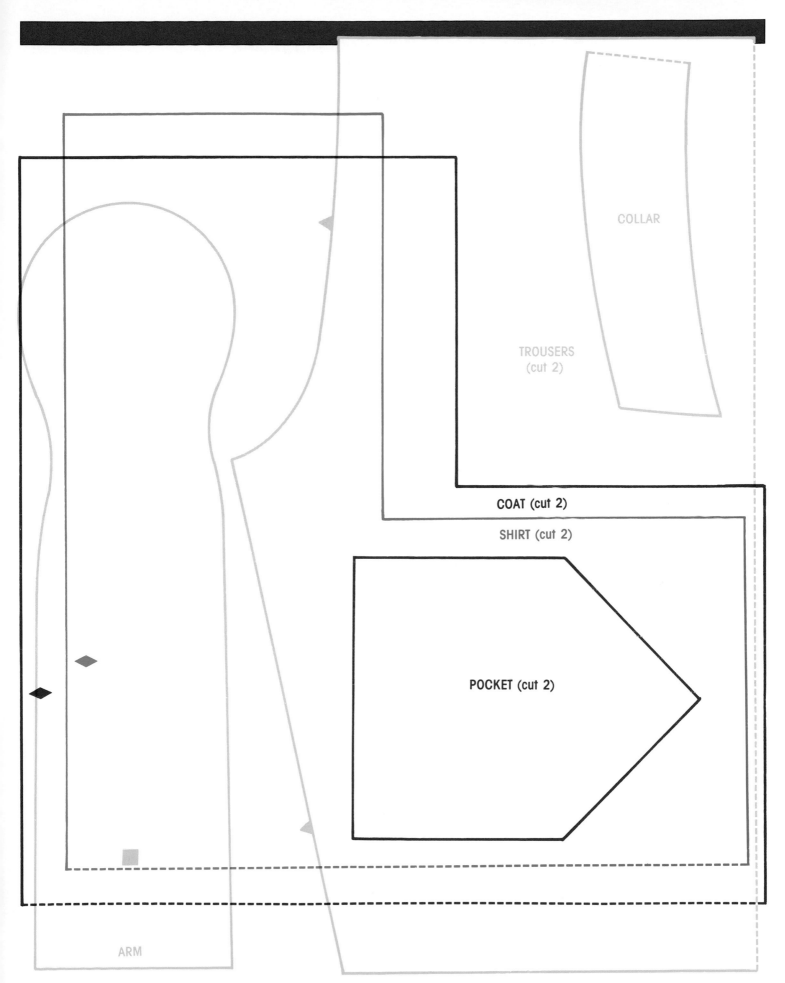

COLLAR

TROUSERS
(cut 2)

COAT (cut 2)

SHIRT (cut 2)

POCKET (cut 2)

ARM

THE SHARING OF CHRISTMAS

One of the greatest joys of Christmas comes from giving gifts to those we love. There's a special delight in crafting our little surprises and wrapping them in festive paper to be opened on Christmas Day. As the colorful packages appear beneath the tree, an air of expectancy fills the house. And when that special morning finally arrives and our treasures are unwrapped, we experience the pleasure of having given from the heart!

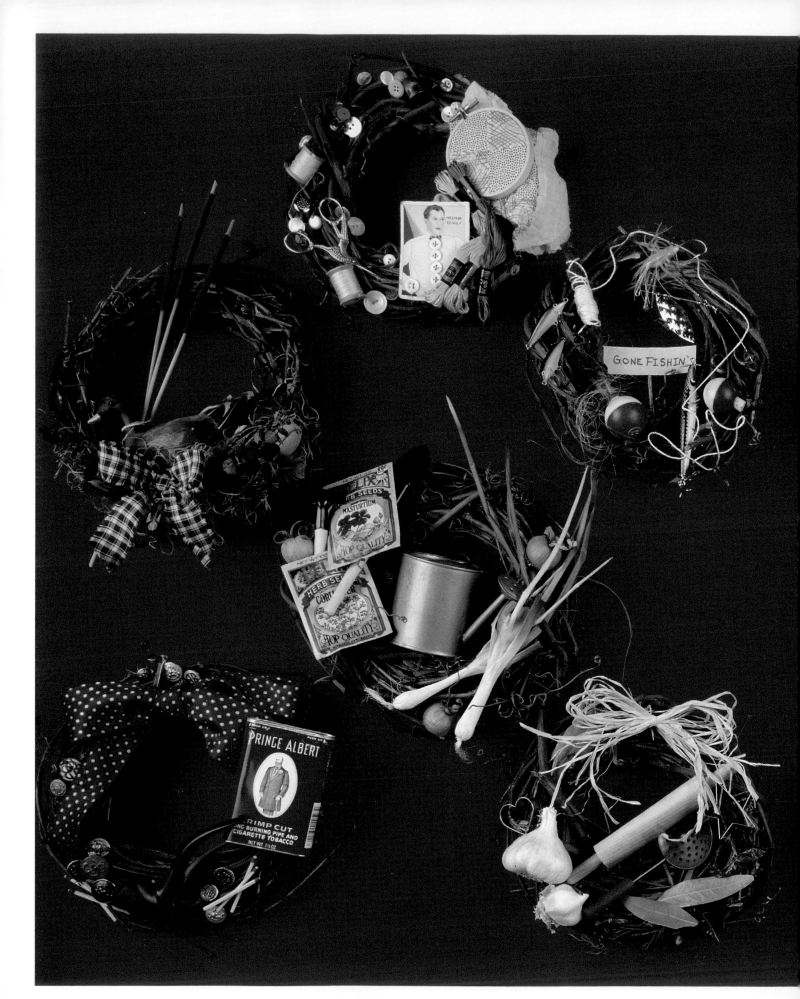

PERSONAL WREATHS

Creating a personalized gift has never been more fun! With a grapevine wreath, a few odds and ends, and a little imagination, you can create a keepsake that will delight anyone on your gift list. For example, a seamstress will love a collection of antique buttons, wooden spools, scissors, and other sewing notions. An avid fisherman will get a kick out of lures, floats, and a ''Gone Fishin' '' sign. And a cook will treasure a wreath decorated with miniature kitchen utensils and dried herbs. We've also pictured ideas for the golfer, artist, baby, teacher, musician, gardener, pipe smoker, and hunter. Because no two people are alike, each wreath will have a charm all its own.

CHRISTMAS TABLE SET

Our "gift-wrapped" table set is the perfect complement to festive dinnerware — and what hostess wouldn't love a set for her holiday table! Easily sewn from rich green fabric, the place mat is trimmed with "ribbons" of Christmas print fabric highlighted with metallic accents. The matching "bow" is really a fanfolded napkin.

For each place mat and napkin, you will need ½ yd of 44"w fabric for place mat, ½ yd of 22"w heavyweight fusible interfacing, ½ yd of 44"w fabric for napkin and place mat trim, and thread to match fabric.

1. For place mat, cut two 13½" x 19" pieces from place mat fabric and one 13" x 18½" piece from interfacing.
2. For place mat top, follow manufacturer's instructions and fuse interfacing to wrong side of one place mat fabric piece.
3. For place mat trim, cut two 2¾" x 14½" strips from trim fabric. Press long edges of strips ¼" to wrong side. Refer to **Fig. 1** to place strips on right side of place mat top; pin in place. Trim short edges of strips even with edges of place mat top. Stitch close to pressed edges of strips.

Fig. 1

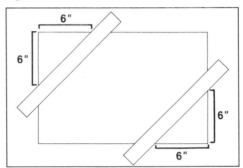

4. For loop to hold napkin, cut one 2¾" x 3½" piece from trim fabric. Press long edges ¼" to wrong side; press ¼" to wrong side again and stitch in place. Press short edges of fabric ¼" to wrong side. Center loop piece on upper left trim strip; whipstitch short edges of loop piece to long edges of trim (**Fig. 2**).

Fig. 2

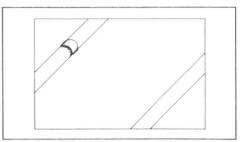

5. With right sides facing and leaving an opening for turning, use a ¼" seam allowance and sew place mat pieces together. Cut corners diagonally and turn right side out; press. Sew final closure by hand. Topstitch ¼" from edges of place mat.
6. For napkin, cut an 18" square from trim fabric. Press all edges ¼" to wrong side; press ¼" to wrong side again and stitch in place.
7. Fold napkin in half and, referring to photo, fanfold napkin. Insert folded napkin through loop to resemble a bow.

FESTIVE CANDLE HOLDERS

Resembling fine marble, these striking candlesticks are actually made from wood and painted with a simple false-graining technique. For a festive gift, attach sprigs of silk holly and present the holders along with a pair of red candles.

For each pair of candlesticks, you will need two 3½" long pieces cut from a two-by-four piece of wood; two 1"h wooden candle cups; two ¾" long wood screws; screwdriver; the following Folk Art™ products: Old Ivy acrylic paint, Blacksmith Black Antiquing, Thickener, and Waterbase Varnish; foam brushes; plastic wrap; medium and fine sandpaper; a small bowl; two sprigs of artificial holly; hot glue gun; and glue sticks.

1. Use medium sandpaper to sand wood pieces.
2. To assemble candlesticks, center one candle cup on each wood piece. Use screws to secure candle cups to wood.
3. Apply one coat of Old Ivy paint to candlesticks; allow to dry. Use fine sandpaper to smooth. Repeat to apply a second coat of paint.
4. For glaze, mix 1 tablespoon Antiquing and 2 tablespoons Thickener in small bowl.
5. Working quickly, apply one coat of glaze to candlesticks so that paint color barely shows through glaze. For mottled effect, refer to photo and use a crumpled piece of plastic wrap to stamp candlesticks; allow to dry.
6. Apply two coats of varnish to candlesticks, allowing to dry between coats.
7. Referring to photo, glue sprigs of holly to candlesticks.

GIFTS FOR HER

This feminine ensemble is a lovely way to keep a dressing table in order. Trimmed with burgundy tassels and twisted satin cord, the padded tray keeps toiletry items close at hand. An ordinary comb, brush, and mirror become elegant accessories when backed with floral fabric and edged with matching cord. The velvet pouch is a luxurious place to store jewelry, and a boutique tissue box cover sewn from floral fabric completes the gift set.

VANITY SET

You will need a comb, brush, and mirror vanity set (a set with little ornamentation works best); fabric, lightweight fusible interfacing, and ⅛" dia. twisted satin cord (amounts determined by sizes of areas to be covered); tracing paper; and fabric glue.

1. To cover back of mirror, place tracing paper on back of mirror; refer to photo and carefully draw around area to be covered with fabric. Cut out pattern.
2. Cut one piece of fabric 1" larger on all sides than pattern; cut one piece of interfacing slightly smaller than fabric piece. Follow manufacturer's instructions to fuse interfacing to wrong side of fabric piece. Use pattern and cut one piece from fabric.

3. Glue fabric piece to back of mirror; allow to dry.

4. For cord trim, carefully measure around area to be covered with cord. To prevent ends of cord from fraying, apply glue to end of cord and to a ½" area where cord will be cut; allow to dry. Cut cord desired length.

5. Glue cord over edge of fabric piece; allow to dry.

6. To cover back of brush, repeat Steps 1 – 5.

7. To cover top of comb, measure length and width of area to be covered and add ½" to each measurement. Cut one fabric piece the determined measurements. Press all edges of fabric ¼" to wrong side. Glue fabric to comb; allow to dry. For cord trim, repeat Step 4; glue cord to comb along fabric edges and allow to dry.

TRAY

You will need one 14" x 20" piece of foam core board, 1¼ yds of 44"w fabric, four 3" long tassels, 3½ yds of ⅛" dia. twisted satin cord, thread to match fabric and tassels, extra-loft polyester bonded batting, removable fabric marking pen, fabric glue, transparent tape, and craft knife.

1. Use craft knife to cut the following pieces from foam core board: one 11" x 17" piece for bottom, two 1" x 17" pieces for long sides, and two 1" x 10½" pieces for short sides.

2. Cut the following pieces from batting: two 11" x 17" pieces for bottom, two 2½" x 17" pieces for long sides, and two 2½" x 10½" pieces for short sides.

3. Glue bottom batting pieces to one side (top) of bottom board piece. Wrap one side batting piece around each side board piece; tape in place.

4. Cut the following pieces from fabric: two 15¾" x 18" pieces for long sides and two 11½" x 22¼" pieces for short sides.

5. (**Note:** Use a ¼" seam allowance throughout. Backstitch at beginning and end of each seam. Cut corners diagonally.) Place long sides fabric pieces right sides together. Sew long edges and one short edge together to form a bag. Press remaining edge ¼" to wrong side. Turn right side out; press. For long sides of tray, refer to **Fig. 1** and use fabric marking pen to draw a line 1¾" from each long edge. Sew along pen lines. Remove pen lines. Insert long side board pieces into side

openings; insert bottom board piece into center opening. Sew final closures by hand.

Fig. 1

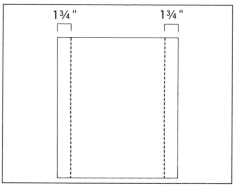

6. Place remaining fabric pieces right sides together. Sew short edges and one long edge together to form a bag. Press remaining raw edge ¼" to wrong side. Turn right side out; press. For short sides of tray, refer to **Fig. 2** and use fabric marking pen to draw a line 1¾" from each short edge. Sew along pen lines. Remove pen lines. Insert short side board pieces into side openings; sew final closures by hand.

Fig. 2

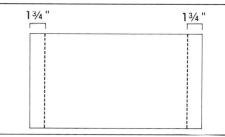

7. To assemble tray, place short sides piece on a flat surface. Referring to **Fig. 3a**, apply glue to top of short sides piece. Referring to **Fig. 3b**, position long sides piece on top of short sides piece. Weight pieces with a heavy book; allow to dry. Referring to photo, fold up sides of tray to meet; whipstitch edges of sides together.

Fig. 3a

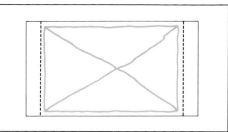

Fig. 3b

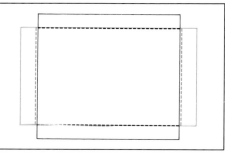

Continued on page 94

Individual pockets sewn into the lining of the elegant jewelry pouch keep cherished pieces neatly organized.

8. For cord trim, refer to photo and follow Step 4 of Vanity Set instructions, page 93, to cut cord to fit inside edges of bottom of tray and outside of tray along seamlines. Glue cord in place; allow to dry.

9. For tassels, knot hanging loop close to tassel and trim ends. Refer to photo and tack one tassel at each corner of tray.

TISSUE BOX COVER

For boutique tissue box cover, you will need one 13" x 20" piece of fabric, lightweight fusible interfacing, thread to match fabric, removable fabric marking pen, 40" of ⅛" dia. twisted satin cord, fabric glue, and one 4½" x 4½" x 5½" box of boutique tissues.

1. Cut the following pieces from fabric: two 2¾" x 5" pieces for top and one 6¼" x 18" piece for sides. Cut pieces from interfacing slightly smaller than fabric pieces. Follow manufacturer's instructions to fuse interfacing to wrong sides of fabric pieces.

2. (**Note:** Use a ¼" seam allowance throughout. Backstitch at beginning and end of each seam.) For top of cover, match right sides and long edges of top pieces; sew two ¾" long seams as shown in **Fig. 1**. Press seam open.

Fig. 1

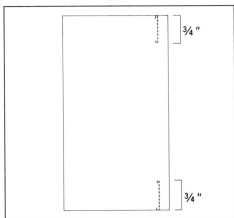

3. For sides of cover, match right sides and short edges of sides piece; sew short edges together to form a tube. Press seam open.

4. Use fabric marking pen to mark a ¼" seam allowance on all edges of top piece and on one raw edge (top) of sides piece.

5. Matching right sides and pen lines, pin top and sides pieces together. To ease sides piece at corners, clip ⅛"

into top edge of sides piece at each corner. Sew top and sides pieces together along pen lines. Remove pen lines.

6. Press bottom edge of cover ¼" to wrong side; press ¼" to wrong side again. Stitch in place. Turn cover right side out.

7. Place cover on box. For cord trim, follow Step 4 of Vanity Set instructions, page 93, and glue cord around cover along top and bottom edges; allow to dry.

JEWELRY POUCH

You will need two 19" squares of velvet or velveteen fabric for outside of pouch, two 14" squares of satin fabric for inside of pouch, size 3 pearl cotton to match velvet fabric, 32" of ⅛" dia. twisted satin cord, two 3" long tassels, thread to match fabrics and tassels, fabric marking pencil, string, ruler, and thumbtack or pin.

1. For outside of pouch, match right sides of one velvet piece and fold in half from top to bottom and again from left to right.

2. To mark cutting line, tie one end of string to fabric marking pencil. Insert thumbtack through string 8½" from pencil. Insert thumbtack in fabric as shown in **Fig. 1** and mark one-fourth of a circle.

Fig. 1

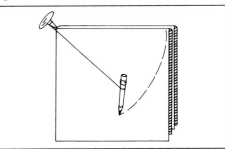

3. Following cutting line and cutting through all thicknesses of fabric, cut out circle. Using circle for a pattern, cut out remaining velvet fabric piece.

4. For inside of pouch, use satin pieces and follow Steps 1 – 3, inserting thumbtack through string 6" from pencil.

5. (**Note:** Use a ½" seam allowance.) With right sides facing and leaving an opening for turning, sew velvet circles together. Repeat for satin circles. Clip curves and trim seam allowances; turn circles right side out and press. Sew final closures by hand.

6. Topstitch ¼" from edge of velvet circle.

7. To divide satin circle into eight sections, fold satin circle in half; fold in half two more times. Use pins to mark folds on edge of circle. Unfold fabric. Using ruler and fabric marking pencil, connect marks to divide circle into sections; remove pins. Use fabric marking pencil and string to draw a 3" dia. circle in center of satin (**Fig. 2**).

Fig. 2

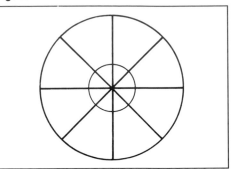

8. To form pockets, center satin circle on velvet circle and pin in place. Thread sewing machine with needle thread to match satin and bobbin thread to match velvet. Sewing through all thicknesses, sew along marked lines and around marked circle.

9. For cord loop, refer to **Fig. 3** and use pearl cotton to come up at one pocket seamline on outside of pouch; go down through fabric ⅜" from seamline. Allowing enough space to insert cord through loop, knot ends of pearl cotton together on inside of pouch; trim ends. Repeat to sew one loop at each pocket seamline.

Fig. 3

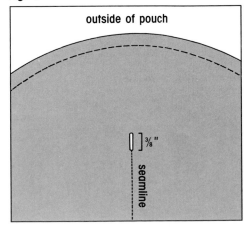

10. Thread cord through loops. Remove hanging loops from tassels and whipstitch tassels to ends of cord.

SANTA SWEATSHIRT

Framed by a wreath of evergreen and holly, a lovable Santa face graces a no-sew appliqué sweatshirt. Fabric paint and glitter outline the fabric pieces, and curled ribbon creates Santa's snowy white beard. What a jolly gift!

You will need one sweatshirt; the following pieces of cotton or cotton blend fabrics: one 9" square of red fabric for berries and hat, one 8" square of lt green fabric and one 8" square of dk green fabric for holly, one 15" square of dk green print fabric for wreath, one 4" square of pink fabric for face, and one 9" x 14" piece of white fabric for eyebrows, tassel, and hat trim/beard; red, green, and iridescent white squeezable fabric paint pens; lightweight fusible interfacing; paper-backed fusible web; small round paintbrush; paper towel; cardboard to fit snugly inside body of sweatshirt; two ⅝" dia. black buttons; black thread; fine white glitter; fine red glitter; tracing paper; appliqué pressing sheet; size 7 metal knitting needles; spring-type wooden clothespins; Unique Stitch™ fabric glue; and 10 yds of ⅛"w white satin ribbon.

1. Wash, dry, and press sweatshirt and fabrics.
2. Cut pieces of interfacing and web slightly smaller than fabric pieces. Follow manufacturer's instructions to fuse interfacing, then web, to wrong sides of fabric pieces.
3. Matching arrows to form one pattern, trace hat trim/beard pattern, pages 96 and 97, onto tracing paper. Trace remaining patterns, pages 96 and 97, onto tracing paper. Cut out patterns.
4. Use patterns and cut out fabric pieces as indicated on pattern. Remove paper backing.
5. (**Note:** Diagram is shown on page 96.) Place appliqué pressing sheet on ironing board. Place hat piece right side up on appliqué pressing sheet.

Refer to Diagram to layer tassel and hat trim/beard piece on hat piece. Follow manufacturer's instructions to fuse pieces together. Refer to Diagram to layer face, then eyebrows on hat trim/beard piece; fuse pieces together.
6. Place sweatshirt on ironing board. Refer to Diagram and photo to layer wreath, holly, and berry pieces on sweatshirt; place Santa piece inside wreath on sweatshirt.
7. Trim any leaves or wreath pieces that are overlapped by beard. Fuse design to sweatshirt. Place cardboard inside sweatshirt.
8. (**Note:** Practice painting technique on scrap of fabric. Make long, even strokes with paint, releasing pressure on pen only when ending a line of paint. Do not use an almost empty paint pen; paint may splatter. For Steps 8 – 10, refer to dashed lines on patterns to paint detail

lines.) Center a thick, even line of red paint over exposed raw edges of berries and hat; paint detail lines on berries. Sprinkle red glitter over wet paint, coating well. Allow paint to dry. Shake off excess glitter.
9. Center a thick, even line of green paint over exposed edges of holly leaves; paint detail lines on leaves. Allow paint to dry.
10. Center a thick, even line of white paint over remaining exposed raw edges of design; paint detail lines on face, hat trim, and beard. Sprinkle white glitter over wet paint, coating well. Allow paint to dry. Shake off excess glitter.
11. For cheeks, dip paintbrush in red fabric paint. Stroke paintbrush on paper towel until almost all the paint is removed. Stroke brush on fabric to blush cheeks.

Continued on page 96

SANTA SWEATSHIRT (continued)

12. Allow sweatshirt to dry for 24 hours.

13. To curl ribbon, cut ribbon in 18" lengths. Wet ribbon. Overlapping long edges, tightly wrap one ribbon length around a knitting needle. Secure ribbon on needle with clothespins. Repeat for remaining needle. Place needles on a cookie sheet and dry in a pre-heated 250 degree oven for approximately 20 minutes or until dry. Repeat for remaining lengths.

14. (**Note:** Glue ribbon lengths as needed to keep ribbon from pulling away from design.) For beard and mustache curls, refer to photo to glue ribbon lengths inside painted lines, trimming ribbon to fit as necessary; allow to dry. Remove cardboard from sweatshirt.

15. For eyes, sew buttons where indicated by **x**'s on pattern.

16. To wash shirt, turn shirt wrong side out and hand wash or machine wash in cool water, using fabric softener in the final rinse. Gently squeeze out excess water. Turn right side out and lay shirt flat to dry.

DIAGRAM

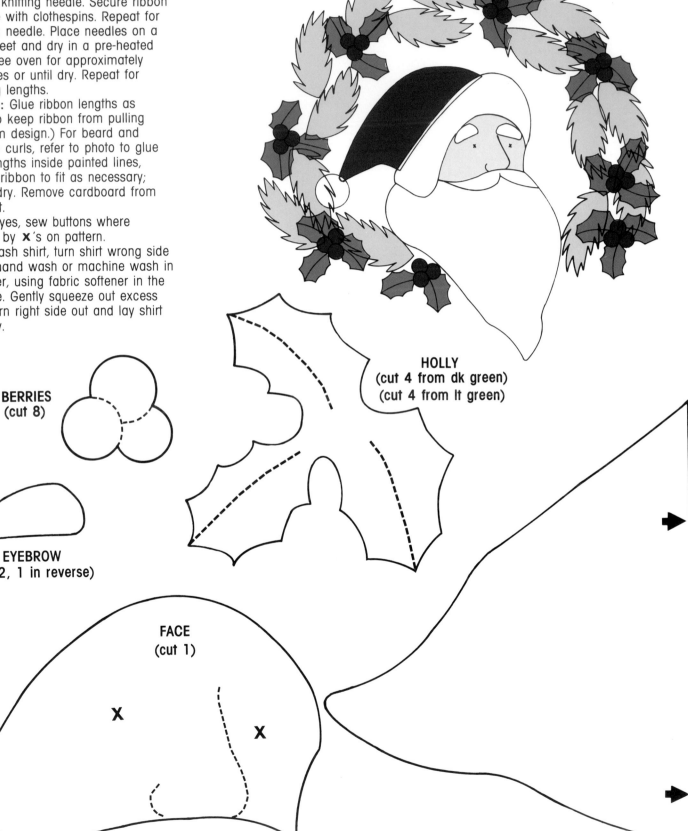

BERRIES
(cut 8)

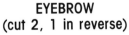

HOLLY
(cut 4 from dk green)
(cut 4 from lt green)

EYEBROW
(cut 2, 1 in reverse)

FACE
(cut 1)

X   X

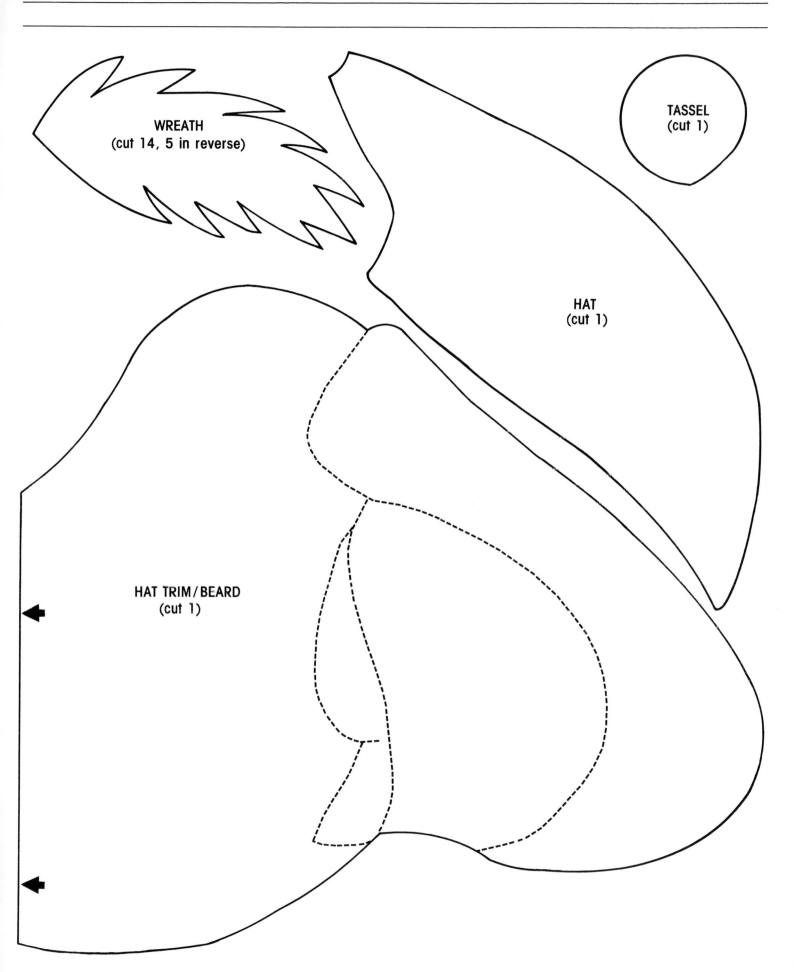

WREATH
(cut 14, 5 in reverse)

TASSEL
(cut 1)

HAT
(cut 1)

HAT TRIM / BEARD
(cut 1)

GIFTS FOR HIM

These handsome gifts are sure to please the man in your life. The fabric-covered frame is an attractive (yet inexpensive) way to showcase a favorite picture. To coordinate with our waterfowl print, we chose fabric sporting an English hunt scene. The potpourri, enhanced with citrus oil, has a fresh, outdoorsy scent. Presented in a crackle-finished box, it will make a nice addition to an office or study.

For frame, you will need desired size picture frame with a flat or slightly curved molding suitable for covering with fabric, fabric to cover frame, metallic gold paint, small round paintbrush, medium weight fusible interfacing, fabric glue, foam brush, craft knife with extra blades, and matte Mod Podge® sealer.

1. Paint areas of frame that will not be covered with fabric.
2. For each side of frame, measure width and length of area of frame molding to be covered; add 2" to each measurement. Cut pieces of fabric the determined measurements.
3. Cut one piece of interfacing slightly smaller than each fabric piece. Following manufacturer's instructions, fuse interfacing to wrong side of each fabric piece.
4. For one side of frame, cut a strip from interfaced fabric the width of the area to be covered.

5. Use foam brush to apply a thin, even coat of glue to area of frame molding to be covered; center fabric strip on molding and lightly press strip into glue to remove any air bubbles. Allow to dry for a few minutes.
6. (**Note:** Replace blade of knife frequently to avoid fraying fabric.) Use craft knife to carefully cut through fabric along miters at corners of frame; discard excess fabric.
7. Repeat Steps 4 — 6 for remaining sides of frame. Allow to dry completely.
8. Apply two coats of sealer to frame, allowing to dry between coats.

For potpourri, you will need sweet gum balls, red eucalyptus, pieces of dried orange peel, almond and hickory nuts in shells, dried sumac, red preserved cedar, preserved greenery, bay leaves, citrus-type essential oil, and a jar with a tight-fitting lid.

GIFTS FOR HIM (continued)

For potpourri box, you will need desired size Shaker box, black and maroon acrylic paint, Deco Art™ Weathered Wood™ crackling medium, paintbrushes, and matte clear acrylic spray.

1. For potpourri, place dry ingredients in jar and add desired amount of oil. Secure lid on jar and place jar in a cool, dark, dry place for two weeks. Every few days, shake jar to mix contents. Add additional oil if desired.
2. For basecoat on box, paint outside of box and lid black; allow to dry.
3. Following manufacturer's instructions, apply Weathered Wood™ and maroon paint to outside of box and lid. Allow to dry.
4. Paint inside of box and lid maroon; allow to dry.
5. Spray box and lid with acrylic spray; allow to dry.
6. Fill box with potpourri.

ELEGANT PILLOWS

Perfect for someone who enjoys elegant accents, these throw pillows make wonderful holiday gifts. The square one, sewn from floral tapestry fabric, is enhanced with plush purchased fringe. The oblong pillow, made of shimmering black moiré, is trimmed with taupe shirred welting for dramatic contrast. Given as a set or alone, these luxurious pillows will dress up any room!

For pillow with fringe, you will need two 16" squares of fabric, 2 yds of 1½"w fringe, thread to match fabric, and polyester fiberfill.

1. (**Note:** Use zipper foot to sew pillow.) Matching bound edge of fringe with raw edge of fabric and clipping fringe at corners if necessary, machine baste fringe to right side of one fabric square; overlap ends of fringe ½".
2. With right sides together and leaving an opening for turning, use a ½" seam allowance and sew fabric squares together. Cut fabric corners diagonally and turn right side out. Stuff pillow with fiberfill; sew final closure by hand.

For pillow with shirred welting, you will need two 14" x 19" pieces of fabric for pillow, one 4½" x 132" strip of fabric for welting (pieced as necessary), 2 yds of 1" dia. cord, thread to match fabrics, and polyester fiberfill.

Continued on page 100

ELEGANT PILLOWS (continued)

1. (**Note:** Use zipper foot to sew welting.) For welting, begin at one end of fabric strip and lay cord along center on wrong side of strip. Matching long edges, fold strip over cord. Insert a pin through welting fabric and end of cord to secure.

2. Machine baste 6" along length of strip close to cord and stop with needle in fabric. Raise presser foot; gently pull cord and push fabric toward pinned end of welting, gathering fabric behind needle (**Fig. 1**). Continue basting and gathering fabric at 6" intervals to end of fabric and cord. Insert a pin through remaining end of fabric and cord to secure. Adjust shirring evenly along length of welting.

Fig. 1

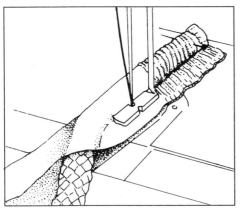

3. Beginning 2" from one end of welting and matching raw edges, machine baste welting to right side of one pillow fabric piece, clipping seam allowance at corners; stop 2" from point where ends of welting overlap.

4. Trim excess welting so ends overlap 1". Remove 1" of basting from one end of welting; open welting fabric and trim 1" from cord. Fold raw edge of welting fabric ½" to wrong side; insert remaining end of welting into trimmed end of welting and tack ends of cord together. Hand baste fabric together and adjust shirring across seam. Machine baste remaining welting to pillow fabric.

5. With right sides together and leaving an opening for turning, use a ½" seam allowance and sew pillow fabric pieces together. Cut corners diagonally and turn pillow right side out. Stuff pillow with fiberfill; sew final closure by hand.

MITTENS FOR KIDS

Kids will love the bright colors and bold stripes of these snuggly mittens! We've given instructions for knitting two sizes, 2-4 and 6-8.

ABBREVIATIONS

K   knit
P   purl
st(s)   stitch(es)
tog   together
PSSO   pass slipped stitch over

( ) — contains explanatory remarks

MATERIALS

For Small Mittens (size 2-4) or Large Mittens (size 6-8), you will need Worsted Weight Yarn, approximately:
Color A (red) — 1 ounce (29 grams, 69 yards)
Color B (blue) — 1 ounce (29 grams, 69 yards)
Color C (green) — 1 ounce (29 grams, 69 yards)
Straight knitting needles, size 7 (4.50 mm) **or** size needed for gauge
2 stitch holders
Markers
Yarn needle

GAUGE: In Stockinette Stitch, 5 sts and 7 rows = 1" DO NOT HESITATE TO CHANGE NEEDLE SIZE TO OBTAIN CORRECT GAUGE.

Note: Instructions are written for small mittens with measurements for large mittens in parentheses.

INSTRUCTIONS
RIGHT MITTEN
CUFF

With Color A, cast on 24 (28) sts **loosely**.
Work in K1, P1 ribbing for 1½" (2").

HAND

Row 1: With Color B, knit across.
Row 2: Purl across.

Thumb Gusset

Row 1 (Increase row): K 14 (16), place marker, work **Right Increase** (slants to the right) as follows: insert right needle into right side of the stitch below that on the left needle (**Fig. 1a**), slip loop onto left needle and knit (**Fig. 1b**) (**Right Increase made**), K1, work **Left Increase** (slants to the left) as follows: insert left needle into the left side of the stitch 2 rows below the stitch just knit, knit through the back loop (**Left Increase made**), place marker, knit across: 26 (30) sts.

Fig. 1a

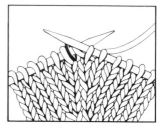

Fig. 1b

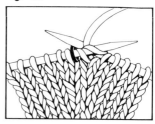

Row 2: Purl across.
Row 3 (Increase row): Knit to marker, slip marker, Right Increase, knit to marker, Left Increase, slip marker, knit across: 28 (32) sts.
Row 4: Purl across.
Repeat Rows 3 and 4, 1 (2) time(s): 30 (36) sts.

Thumb

Dividing Row: Knit to marker and slip those sts onto st holder, remove marker, knit to marker, remove marker, Left Increase, slip remaining sts on left needle onto second st holder: 8 (10) sts. Work even until thumb measures approximately 1" (1½") **or to desired length**, ending by working a **purl** row.
Decrease Row: K2 tog across: 4 (5) sts. Cut yarn leaving a 12" end. Thread yarn needle with end and weave through remaining sts, pulling firmly to close; weave seam.

Top

Row 1: With **right** side facing, slip sts from first st holder onto needle, slip sts from second st holder onto second needle, **Make One** as follows: insert right needle under the bar before the next

stitch (between stitches) (**Fig. 2**), wrap the yarn around the needle and pull it through, making a stitch on the needle (**Make One completed**), knit across: 24 (28) sts.

Fig. 2

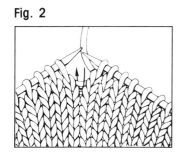

Row 2: Purl across.
Work in Stockinette St (knit 1 row, purl 1 row) for 4 (6) rows. With Color C, work even in Stockinette St until mitten measures approximately 5" (6½") from cast on edge **or to desired length**, ending by working a **purl** row.

Top Shaping
Row 1 (Decrease row): K1, slip 1 as if to **knit**, K1, PSSO, K7 (9), K2 tog, K1, slip 1 as if to **knit**, K1, PSSO, K6 (8), K2 tog, K1: 20 (24) sts.
Row 2 (Decrease row): P1, P2 tog, P4 (6), work **Purl Decrease** (**abbreviated PD**) as follows: P1, slip last st worked back onto left needle, slip second st on left needle over first st, slip completed st back onto right needle (**PD made**), P1, P2 tog, P5 (7), PD, P1: 16 (20) sts.
Row 3 (Decrease row): K1, slip 1 as if to **knit**, K1, PSSO, K3 (5), K2 tog, K1, slip 1 as if to **knit**, K1, PSSO, K2 (4), K2 tog, K1: 12 (16) sts.
Row 4 (Decrease row): P1, P2 tog, P 0 (2), PD, P1, P2 tog, P1 (3), PD, P1: 8 (12) sts.

Size 6-8 ONLY
Row 5 (Decrease row): K1, slip 1 as if to **knit**, K1, PSSO, K1, K2 tog, K1, slip 1 as if

to **knit**, K1, PSSO, K2 tog, K1: (8) sts.

Cut yarn leaving a 20" end. Thread yarn needle with end and weave through remaining sts, pulling firmly to close; weave seam.

LEFT MITTEN
Work same as Right Mitten to Thumb Gusset.

Thumb Gusset
Row 1 (Increase row): K9 (11), place marker, Right Increase, K1, Left Increase, place marker, knit across: 26 (30) sts. Work same as Right Mitten, beginning with **Row 2**.

YEARBOOK SHIRT

This yearbook shirt is a fun way to preserve highlights of the school year for a special teen. Sporting pictures of friends and campus activities, the keepsake shirt is created with a simple transfer technique using photocopies and a special glue. Messages and other finishing details are added using fabric paint pens.

Note: Photographs with darker backgrounds work well for this project. If using photographs with light backgrounds, add a dark border to photocopies to help the photos stand out. Words and numbers will be reversed; use photos without letters or numbers if possible. Photocopies should be as clear as possible.

You will need one light-colored sweatshirt, black and white or color photocopies of photographs, Slomon's Stitchless Fabric Glue, removable fabric marking pen, foam brush, squeezable fabric paint pens, waxed paper, cardboard cut to fit snugly inside body of sweatshirt, pressing cloth, and a brayer or rolling pin.

1. Wash, dry, and press sweatshirt. Place cardboard inside shirt.
2. Lay photocopies face down in desired position on shirt. If photocopies overlap, trim overlapping area from one photocopy.
3. Use fabric marking pen to lightly mark placement of corners of photocopies. Remove photocopies.
4. To make transfers, use foam brush to apply an even coat of glue to front of each photocopy so that the image of the photocopy barely shows through glue.
5. Without touching glue, place photocopies glue side down where marked on shirt.
6. Cover photocopies with waxed paper. Firmly roll brayer over photocopies to remove air bubbles. Remove waxed paper and allow to dry for 24 hours.
7. Heat set transfers using pressing cloth and a hot, dry iron.
8. To remove paper from sweatshirt, brush a liberal amount of warm water across one photocopy; allow water to stand for several minutes. Working from center to outside edges, use fingers to gently roll a thin layer of paper off of transfer (transfer will appear cloudy). Adding water as necessary, repeat until all paper has been removed and transfer is as clear as original photocopy. Repeat for remaining transfers. Allow to dry.
9. To seal transfers, mix 1 part glue to 1 part water. Apply a thin coat of glue mixture over each transfer. Allow to dry.
10. Refer to photo and use fabric marking pen to lightly write desired words or draw desired designs. Use paint pens to draw over pen lines. Allow to dry.
11. Hand wash shirt wrong side out in cold water. Turn right side out and lay flat to dry. Iron on wrong side.

BATH BASKET

Colorful hand towels embroidered with pulled thread stitches make nice holiday accents for the bath. For an attractive gift basket, present a pair of these pretty towels along with some fancy soaps.

FOUR-SIDED STITCH
Fig. 1

HERRINGBONE STITCH
Fig. 2

DIAMOND EYELET STITCH
Fig. 3

For each towel, you will need one prefinished fingertip towel with 14 count insert and desired colors of embroidery floss.

(**Note:** Refer to chart and **Figs. 1**, **2**, and **3** to work designs.) With design centered between long edges of insert, use 2 strands of floss to work design across entire insert, repeating as necessary.

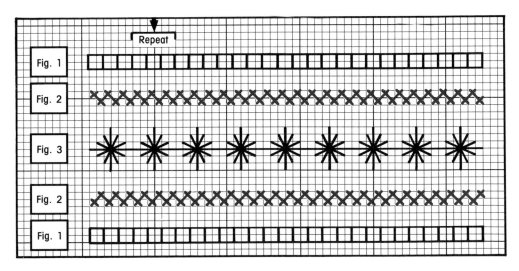

Repeat

Fig. 1
Fig. 2
Fig. 3
Fig. 2
Fig. 1

COZY WRAP

This handsome afghan is sure to warm hearts (and toes!) on Christmas morning. Crocheted with two strands of yarn, it's extra cozy — and quick to make, too.

Finished Size: approximately 54" x 66"

ABBREVIATIONS
CC   Contrasting Color
ch(s)   chain(s)
hdc   half double crochet(s)
MC   Main Color
tr   treble crochet(s)

★ — work instructions following ★ as many **more** times as indicated in addition to the first time.
( ) — contains explanatory remarks.

MATERIALS
Worsted Weight Yarn, approximately:
  MC — 42 ounces,
    (1200 grams, 2640 yards)
  CC — 39 ounces,
    (1114 grams, 2451 yards)
Crochet hook, size N (9.00 mm)
  or size needed for gauge

GAUGE: Working double strand,
    13 tr and 4 rows = 6".
    DO NOT HESITATE TO CHANGE
    HOOK SIZE TO OBTAIN
    CORRECT GAUGE.

Note: Entire Afghan is worked holding two strands of yarn together.

INSTRUCTIONS
With 2 strands of MC, ch 123 **loosely.**
Row 1 (Right side): Hdc in 4th ch from hook and in next ch, tr in next 4 chs, ★ hdc in next 4 chs, tr in next 4 chs; repeat from ★ across to last 2 chs, hdc in last 2 chs: 120 sts.

Note: Loop a short piece of yarn around any stitch to mark last row as **right** side.
Row 2: Ch 3, turn (counts as beginning hdc now and throughout); hdc in next hdc, tr in next 4 tr, ★ hdc in next 4 hdc, tr in next 4 tr; repeat from ★ across to last 2 hdc, hdc in last 2 hdc.
Row 3: With 2 strands of CC, ch 4, turn (counts as beginning tr now and throughout); tr in next hdc, hdc in next 4 tr, ★ tr in next 4 hdc, hdc in next 4 tr; repeat from ★ across to last 2 hdc, tr in last 2 hdc.
Row 4: Ch 4, turn; tr in next tr, hdc in next 4 hdc, ★ tr in next 4 tr, hdc in next 4 hdc; repeat from ★ across to last 2 tr, tr in last 2 tr.
Row 5: With 2 strands MC, ch 3, turn; hdc in next tr, tr in next 4 hdc, ★ hdc in next 4 tr, tr in next 4 hdc; repeat from ★ across to last 2 tr; hdc in last 2 tr.
Rows 6-62: Repeat Rows 2-5 fourteen times; work Row 2; finish off.

CHRISTMAS SWEATSHIRT

With its heartfelt verse, this cross-stitched sweatshirt will kindle holiday spirits. You'll want to give the shirt early so it can be enjoyed throughout the season.

You will need one sweatshirt, embroidery floss (see color key), 13" x 12" piece of 8.5 mesh waste canvas, 13" x 12" piece of lightweight non-fusible interfacing, masking tape, #24 tapestry needle, embroidery hoop (optional), tweezers, and a spray bottle filled with water.

1. Wash, dry, and press sweatshirt. Cover edges of canvas with masking tape.
2. Refer to photo for placement of design; mark center of design on sweatshirt with a straight pin.
3. Match center of canvas to pin. Use blue threads in canvas to place canvas straight on sweatshirt; pin canvas to sweatshirt. Pin interfacing to wrong side of sweatshirt under canvas. Baste securely around edges of canvas through all three thicknesses. Then baste from corner to corner and from side to side.
4. (**Note:** Using a hoop is recommended when working on a sweatshirt.) Work design on canvas, stitching from large holes to large holes. Use 6 strands of floss for Cross Stitch, 6 for Backstitch, and 2 for French Knots.
5. Remove basting threads and trim canvas to within ¾" of design. Spray canvas with water until it becomes limp. Pull out canvas threads one at a time using tweezers.
6. Trim interfacing close to design.

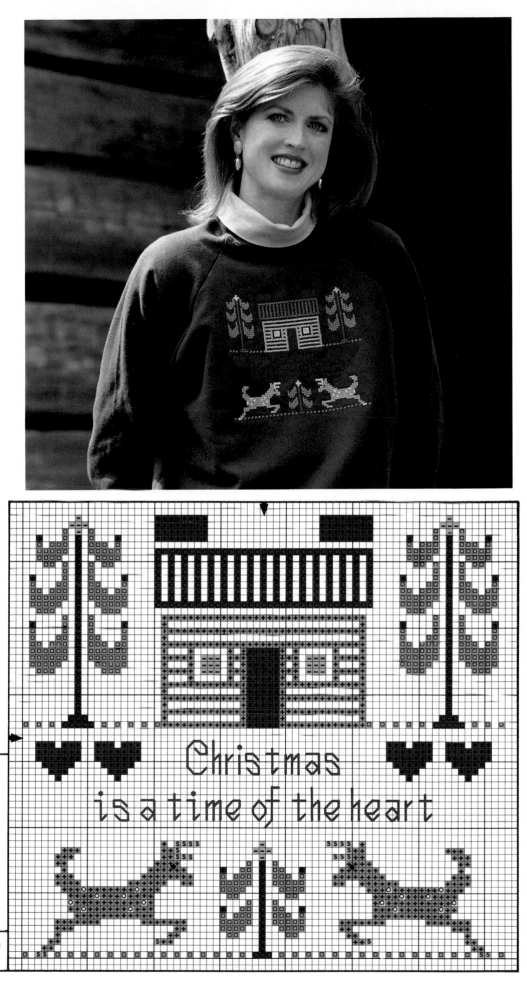

TIME OF THE HEART (73w x 67h)

X	DMC	B'ST	ANC.	COLOR
⊙	ecru		0387	ecru
✱	321	◲	047	red
■	433		0944	brown
+	436		0360	tan
▣	562		0205	green
S	648		0398	grey
–	725		028	yellow
•	black French Knot			
•	red French Knot			

Design size worked over 8.5 mesh waste canvas — 8⅝" x 8".

MERRY JEWELRY

Our easy-to-make Santa jewelry is a fun way to spread holiday cheer! Whether given individually or as a set, the earrings, pin, scarf pendant, and necklace will add merriment to the season.

You will need Sculpey modeling compound; waxed paper; tracing paper; paring knife; desired colors of acrylic paint; paintbrushes; a soft cloth; dk brown water-based stain; matte clear acrylic spray; hot glue gun, glue sticks, and earring posts and backs or clips (for earrings); hot glue gun, glue sticks, and 1" long pin back (for pin); one 6" x 36" bias strip of desired fabric (for pendant); and two ⅝" dia. painted wooden beads, two 1" long pieces of ½" dia. cinnamon stick, and one 1½" x 38" strip of desired fabric (for necklace).

1. Trace desired pattern, page 108, onto tracing paper and cut out.
2. On waxed paper, pat out a ¼" thick piece of modeling compound slightly larger than pattern. Place pattern on modeling compound and use knife to cut out. Carefully lift piece from paper and use fingers to smooth edges.
3. For loop on necklace or pendant, form a ¼" thick 2" long roll from modeling compound. On back of piece, attach one end of roll ½" from top center. Attach remaining end of roll ½" below attached end to form a loop.
4. Follow manufacturer's instructions to harden modeling compound. Allow to cool.
5. Refer to photo to paint piece; allow to dry. Apply stain to piece; remove excess with soft cloth. Allow to dry.
6. Spray piece with acrylic spray; allow to dry.
7. For earrings, glue posts or clips to back of each jewelry piece. For pin, glue pin back to back of jewelry piece. For pendant, thread jewelry piece onto fabric strip and knot ends together. For necklace, refer to photo and thread jewelry piece, cinnamon sticks, and beads onto fabric strip, knotting strip after each addition; knot ends together.

Patterns on page 108

STENCILED GIFTS

With our colorful yuletide stencils, you can dress up holiday gifts or even create your own Christmas cards! Our friendly snowman adds charm to a fabric gift bag, and the plump Santa graces a Shaker box and a book for listing gifts and wishes. Adorned with the heart tree, a plain note card is transformed into a warm holiday greeting.

For book, you will need one approx. 5½"w x 8¼"h cloth-bound book with blank pages, gesso, small flat paintbrush, foam brush, and water-based varnish.

For note card, you will need one approx. 4½" x 5" note card with matching envelope.

For Shaker box, you will need one 5¾" x 7" oval Shaker box, desired water-based stain, fine sandpaper, and water-based varnish.

For gift bag, you will need two 9" x 15½" pieces of fabric, thread to match fabric, 26" of 3-ply jute, two 1"w painted wooden hearts, and craft glue.

You will also need acetate sheets (available at craft or art stores), craft knife, acrylic paint (see photo for colors), removable tape (optional), stencil brushes, black permanent felt-tip pen with fine point, paper towels, and cutting mat or a thick layer of newspapers.

BASIC STENCILING

1. For each color in stencil key, page 109, you will need a piece of acetate 1" larger than pattern on all sides. Place first piece of acetate over pattern and use pen to trace the outlines of areas with the same color. For placement lines, outline remaining areas with dashed lines. Using a new sheet of acetate for each color, repeat for remaining areas on pattern.

2. Place each acetate piece on cutting mat and use craft knife to cut out stencils along solid lines.

3. (**Note:** Stencil key lists the order in which stencils should be used.) Hold or tape stencil in place. Use a clean, dry stencil brush for each color of paint. Dip brush in paint and remove excess paint on a paper towel. Brush should be almost dry to produce good results.

4. Beginning at edge of one cut out area of stencil, apply paint in a stamping motion. Shade design by applying more paint around edge of area than in center. Additional shading may be added by stamping around edge of area with a darker shade of paint. Carefully remove stencil; allow to dry. Repeat for remaining stencils.

Continued on page 108

PROJECT INSTRUCTIONS

1. For book, apply two coats of gesso to cloth part of book, allowing to dry between coats. Paint cloth part of book desired color; allow to dry. Follow Basic Stenciling, page 107, to stencil Santa design in center of book with bottom of design 2" from bottom of book. Refer to photo and use flat paintbrush to paint "Gifts and Wishes" below Santa. Seal painted part of book with two coats of varnish, allowing to dry between coats.

2. For note card, follow Basic Stenciling, page 107, to stencil tree design in center of card.

3. For Shaker box, stain box desired color; allow to dry. Lightly sand box. Apply varnish to box and allow to dry. Follow Basic Stenciling, page 107, to stencil Santa design in center of box lid. Seal box with one coat of varnish; allow to dry.

4. For gift bag, follow Basic Stenciling, page 107, to stencil snowman design in

center of one piece of fabric with bottom of design 2¾" from one short edge of fabric. With right sides facing and matching raw edges, use a ½" seam allowance and sew side and bottom edges of fabric pieces together. Cut corners diagonally. Turn right side out. Press top edge of bag ½" to wrong side; press ½" to wrong side again. Stitch in place. Glue hearts to ends of jute. Tie jute in a bow around bag.

MERRY JEWELRY (continued)

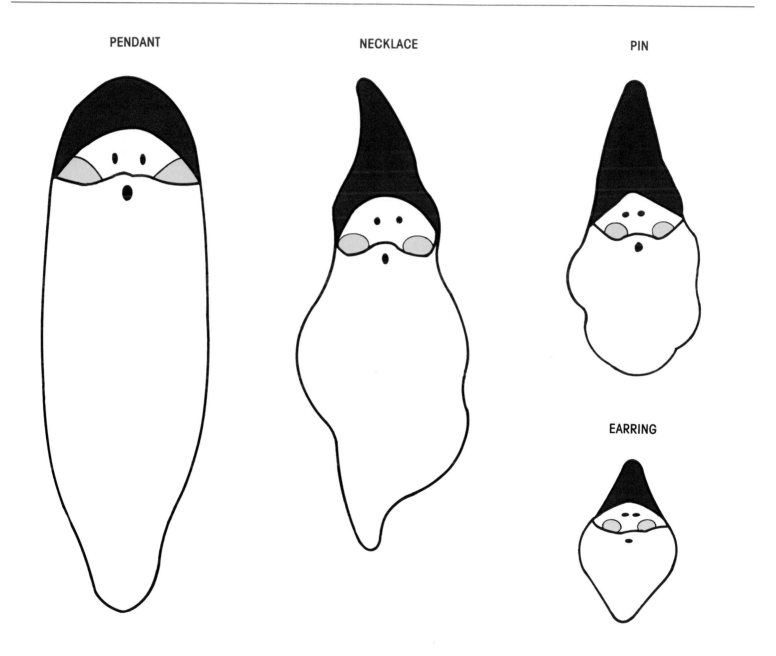

PENDANT NECKLACE PIN

EARRING

STENCIL KEY
#1 ■
#2 □
#3 ■
#4 ■

STENCIL KEY
#1 □
#2 ■
#3 ■

STENCIL KEY
#1 ■
#2 ■
#3 ■

THE TASTES OF CHRISTMAS

As Christmas approaches, our kitchens buzz with excitement and activity. Drawn by tempting aromas, even the little ones want to join in on the fun of holiday baking. Happy chatter fills the room as we sample the goodies that we've come to associate with this wonderful time of year. Served to family and friends or wrapped in festive gift packages, our offerings from the kitchen send delicious Christmas greetings!

American Heritage Dinner

For many of us, the holiday season begins at Thanksgiving and continues throughout the month of December. During this time, we reflect upon our traditions and often find ourselves drawn to the celebrations of years past. Many of our favorite holiday dishes today are simple, hearty foods that have been handed down to us from the American colonists. In honor of this rich heritage, our dinner menu — appropriate for both Christmas and Thanksgiving — offers you a taste of early America.

A succulent Roast Turkey *(left)* accompanied by Cornbread Dressing with Dried Fruit will be enjoyed by all. A traditional English dish, Christmas Chicken Pie is a delicious way to dress up everyday fare.

ROAST TURKEY

- 1 turkey (12 to 14 pounds)
  Salt and freshly ground pepper
- ¼ cup butter, softened
- 2 cups apple cider

Preheat oven to 350 degrees. Remove giblets from turkey and discard or reserve for another use. Rinse turkey and pat dry with paper towels. Liberally salt and pepper turkey inside and out. Tie ends of legs to tail with kitchen twine; lift wing tips up and over back so they are tucked under bird. Place on rack in roasting pan with breast side up. Insert meat thermometer into thickest part of thigh without touching bone. Pour 1 cup water into the pan. Spread butter over turkey. Baste with some of the apple cider. Loosely cover with aluminum foil and roast 2½ hours. Remove foil from turkey. Reduce heat to 325 degrees. Roast uncovered until done (about 1 hour), basting often with apple cider. To test for doneness, meat thermometer should register 180 degrees, or the juices should run clear when the thickest part of the thigh is pierced with a fork. Remove from oven and allow turkey to stand 20 minutes before carving.

Yield: 10 to 12 servings

CORNBREAD DRESSING WITH DRIED FRUIT

- 1½ cups dried mixed fruit bits
- ½ cup butter
- 1 medium onion, chopped
- 1 cup chopped celery
- 5 cups cornbread crumbs
- 2 cups white bread crumbs
- 1½ cups chicken broth
- 1½ teaspoons rubbed sage
- 1 teaspoon poultry seasoning
- 1 teaspoon salt
- ½ teaspoon freshly ground pepper
- 1 egg, lightly beaten

Place fruit in a bowl and add water to bowl to cover fruit. Cover and allow fruit to sit at room temperature overnight.

Preheat oven to 350 degrees. Melt butter in skillet. Add onion and celery and sauté until onion is transparent. Remove from heat and set aside.

Drain fruit. In a large mixing bowl, combine fruit, sautéed mixture, all bread crumbs, and chicken broth. Add sage, poultry seasoning, salt, and pepper, adjusting seasoning as desired. Stir in egg.

Place stuffing in a lightly greased 2-quart baking dish. Cover with aluminum foil and bake 25 to 30 minutes or until stuffing is heated through.

Yield: about 10 servings

CHRISTMAS CHICKEN PIE

CRUST
- 3 cups all-purpose flour
- 1½ teaspoons salt
- 1 cup butter
- ¼ cup ice water

FILLING
- 8 chicken breasts
- ¼ cup butter
- ¼ cup all-purpose flour
- 2½ cups chicken broth
- 1½ teaspoons salt
- ½ teaspoon freshly ground pepper
- 1 teaspoon ground thyme
- 1 teaspoon marjoram flakes
- 1 teaspoon rubbed sage
- 1 pound pork sausage, browned
- 5 slices bacon, cooked and broken into 1-inch pieces
- 1 egg yolk
- 1 teaspoon water

For crust, sift flour and salt into a mixing bowl. Using a pastry blender or two knives, cut butter into flour until mixture resembles coarse meal. Sprinkle water over dough, mixing quickly just until dough forms a ball. Divide dough in half. Press one half of dough into the bottom and up the sides of a lightly greased 2-quart round baking dish. Cover top with plastic wrap. Wrap remaining dough in plastic wrap and refrigerate baking dish and remaining dough until needed.

In a large stockpot, poach chicken breasts in salted boiling water. Remove from water and cool. Remove meat from bone and tear into bite-sized pieces.

For gravy, melt butter in a large saucepan over medium heat. Stir in flour. Stirring constantly, cook until mixture thickens and bubbles. Gradually stir in chicken broth. Stir in salt, pepper, thyme, marjoram, and sage. Cook, stirring constantly, until mixture thickens (3 to 4 minutes).

Preheat oven to 325 degrees. On a lightly floured surface, use a floured rolling pin to roll out remaining dough. Layer half of chicken in bottom of dough-lined baking dish. Layer sausage

Johnnycakes (also called Journey Cakes) were early American favorites.

and bacon over top of chicken. Top with remaining chicken. Pour gravy over meat. Top with rolled dough. Trim dough and crimp edges of pie. Cut slits in top of pie for steam to escape. (If desired, roll out dough scraps and use a cookie cutter to cut out a decoration for top of pie. Apply cutout to pie with a small amount of egg yolk.) Bake 1½ hours. Combine egg yolk with water and brush over top of crust. Bake 5 minutes more.

Yield: about 8 servings

JOHNNYCAKES

- 4 cups cornmeal
- 3 cups boiling water
- ¼ cup firmly packed brown sugar
- 2 tablespoons butter, softened
- 1 teaspoon salt
- 2 eggs, lightly beaten

  Butter and maple syrup or molasses to serve

Preheat oven to 400 degrees. In a medium mixing bowl, combine cornmeal and water, stirring well by hand (mixture will be very thick). Stir in remaining ingredients. Using about ½ cup mixture for each cake, spread mixture into circles about 4 inches in diameter on greased baking sheets. Bake 20 to 25 minutes or until centers are set. Serve warm with butter and maple syrup or molasses.

Yield: 10 to 12 Johnnycakes

CORN CHOWDER

¼ pound salt pork, skin removed and thinly sliced
1 medium onion, chopped
2 large baking potatoes, peeled and chopped
3 cups water, divided
1 cup finely crushed cracker crumbs
3 cups milk
1 can (17 ounces) creamed corn
1½ teaspoons salt
1 teaspoon ground nutmeg

In a large saucepan, fry salt pork with onion until pork is crisp and browned. Stir in potatoes and 2 cups water. Cook over medium heat until potatoes are tender. Combine cracker crumbs and milk and stir into potato mixture. Stir in corn, salt, nutmeg, and remaining 1 cup water. Reduce heat to medium-low and cook, stirring occasionally, 10 minutes or until heated through.
Yield: about 8½ cups of chowder

Savory Corn Chowder makes a satisfying light meal or first course. We used a pumpkin and acorn squash halves for our soup tureen and bowls.

COMPOUND SALLET

DRESSING
1 cup olive oil
⅓ cup red wine vinegar
2 tablespoons granulated sugar

SALAD
2 bunches fresh spinach, rinsed and torn into pieces
1 cup currants
1 cup chopped canned red beets
1 lemon, thinly sliced, rind and seeds removed
1 cup toasted slivered almonds
¼ cup drained capers

Combine dressing ingredients in a jar with a tight-fitting lid. Close jar and shake vigorously to blend.

Toss salad ingredients together in serving bowl. Before serving, pour dressing over salad and toss.
Yield: about 8 servings

Compound Sallet, a flavorful medley of fresh spinach, beets, lemons, nuts, and berries, is complemented by a vinaigrette dressing. In colonial times, the lemon slices would have been a special treat.

Apples and chestnuts complement a traditional holiday vegetable in Sweet Potatoes and Chestnuts *(left)*. Once a favorite colonial party beverage, Sack Posset is a warm custard drink with sherry. Buttery Sweet Potato Pudding is best served with lots of whipped cream.

SWEET POTATO PUDDING

    1 pound sweet potatoes, peeled and
        cut into chunks
    6 eggs, lightly beaten
    3 cups confectioners sugar
 1½ cups butter, softened
    1 teaspoon ground cinnamon
    1 teaspoon ground nutmeg
  ½ teaspoon grated lemon peel
  ½ cup brandy
  ½ cup firmly packed brown sugar

    1 cup whipping cream
    2 tablespoons granulated sugar

In a large saucepan, boil sweet potatoes in water until tender. Drain potatoes and mash until smooth.

Preheat oven to 375 degrees. In a large mixing bowl, combine mashed potatoes, eggs, confectioners sugar, butter, cinnamon, nutmeg, lemon peel, and brandy; blend well. Pour mixture into a greased 13 x 9 x 2-inch baking pan. Bake 40 to 45 minutes or until top is firm. Sprinkle brown sugar over top and bake 5 minutes more.

In a mixing bowl, beat cream with sugar until stiff peaks form. Serve whipped cream with pudding.
Yield: about 12 servings

SWEET POTATOES AND CHESTNUTS

Rich chestnuts have a nutty, earthy flavor that brings out the best in apples and sweet potatoes. Look in gourmet specialty stores to find the canned variety.

    6 large sweet potatoes
    3 apples, peeled, cored, and sliced
    1 can (15.5 ounces) whole chestnuts
        packed in water, drained
  ¾ cup firmly packed brown sugar
    2 teaspoons ground nutmeg
  ¼ cup butter
    1 cup apple cider

In a large saucepan, boil unpeeled sweet potatoes until tender (about 20 minutes). Remove from water and allow to cool.

Preheat oven to 350 degrees. Peel and slice sweet potatoes. In a lightly greased 13 x 9 x 2-inch baking pan, layer sweet potato slices, apples, and chestnuts. Sprinkle top with brown sugar and nutmeg; dot with butter. Pour apple cider over top. Bake 45 minutes or until mixture is bubbly.
Yield: 8 to 10 servings

SACK POSSET

Give this unusual combination of flavors a try on a cold winter's night. Skeptical taste-testers fell in love with the warm, sweet smoothness of this beverage after just one sip!

    1 cup granulated sugar
    1 cup cream sherry
    1 whole nutmeg
    2 cups milk
    5 egg yolks, lightly beaten

In a saucepan, combine sugar, sherry, and nutmeg. Bring to a boil and cook until sugar dissolves; set aside.

In a large saucepan, scald milk. Beat about ½ cup milk into egg yolks; then beat in remaining milk. Return mixture to pan and cook, stirring constantly, over medium-low heat until mixture coats the back of a metal spoon. Gradually stir sherry mixture into milk mixture, blending well. Stirring occasionally, cook over low heat until heated through. Serve warm.
Yield: 4 to 6 servings

CABBAGE WITH RAISINS

   1 head (about 2 pounds) purple
       cabbage, quartered
  ½ cup raisins
  ¼ cup butter
  ¼ cup apple cider vinegar
  2 tablespoons firmly packed brown
       sugar

Fill a large saucepan with salted water and bring to a boil. Add cabbage; cover and cook until tender. Remove from heat and drain water. Using a large spoon, separate leaves of cabbage. Stir in remaining ingredients. Return saucepan to medium heat and cook 5 minutes.
Yield: 4 to 6 servings

ALMOND FLUMMERY

  3 egg yolks
  2 cups whipping cream
  ¾ cup zwieback cracker crumbs
  ½ cup almond paste
  2 tablespoons granulated sugar
  2 tablespoons rose flower water
       (available at gourmet specialty
       stores)
  ¼ teaspoon ground cinnamon
  ¼ teaspoon ground nutmeg
  ¾ cup golden raisins
  ¼ cup toasted slivered almonds

SWEETENED WHIPPED CREAM

  1 cup whipping cream
  2 tablespoons granulated sugar

Preheat oven to 350 degrees. In a large mixing bowl, beat egg yolks with 2 cups cream until well blended. Stir in crumbs and allow to sit 5 minutes to soften. Blend in almond paste, 2 tablespoons sugar, rose flower water, cinnamon, and nutmeg. Stir in raisins. Sprinkle almonds in bottom of a lightly greased 1-quart metal ring mold. Pour mixture into mold. Cover top of mold tightly with aluminum foil. Place mold in a larger pan and add water to larger pan to come halfway up side of mold. Bake 1 hour. Remove from oven and allow to cool 15 minutes in water bath. Remove mold from water bath; remove foil. Allow to cool at room temperature 15 minutes more. Unmold onto serving platter.

Whip 1 cup cream with 2 tablespoons sugar until stiff peaks form. Serve whipped cream with Flummery.
Yield: 8 to 10 servings

The subtle sweet-and-sour flavor of Cabbage with Raisins will be a welcome addition to a holiday meal. It's especially colorful in a hollowed-out pumpkin.

A traditional English steamed pudding served with sweetened whipped cream, Almond Flummery will delight you with its delicious blend of almonds and raisins.

Moist and fruity Ginger Custard makes a wonderful, lightly sweet side dish. We garnished it with a barley sugar Indian. The hearty Baked Beans are laced with maple syrup and molasses.

PLUM CUSTARD

CRUST
- 1½ cups all-purpose flour
- ½ teaspoon salt
- ½ cup butter

FILLING
- 1 can (1 pound) whole, pitted plums in heavy syrup, drained
- ½ cup granulated sugar
- 1 teaspoon ground cinnamon
- 1½ cups half and half
- 2 eggs, lightly beaten

Preheat oven to 350 degrees. For crust, sift flour and salt into a mixing bowl. Using a pastry blender or two knives, cut butter into flour until mixture resembles coarse meal. Using the back of a spoon, firmly press mixture into the bottom and halfway up the sides of a lightly greased 8-inch square baking pan.

Layer plums over crust. Sprinkle sugar and cinnamon over plums. Bake 20 minutes.

In a bowl, blend half and half with eggs. Pour over plums. Bake 30 to 35 minutes or until custard is firm around edges but still slightly soft in center. Custard will firm as it cools. Serve warm or cold.

Yield: about 9 servings

BAKED BEANS

- 2 cups dried navy beans
- 4 cups water
- 1 medium onion, chopped
- 2 tablespoons butter
- ½ cup molasses
- ½ cup maple syrup
- 2 teaspoons salt
- 1 teaspoon dry mustard
- ½ teaspoon ground cinnamon
- 1 teaspoon ground ginger

Cover beans with water and allow to soak overnight.

Drain beans and combine with 4 cups water in a 2-quart saucepan. Bring to a boil over high heat. Cover beans, reduce heat, and simmer 2 hours. Drain beans, reserving 2 cups liquid (add additional water to equal 2 cups if necessary).

In a small skillet, sauté onion in butter until onion is limp. Preheat oven to 350 degrees. In a lightly greased 2-quart baking dish, combine beans, sautéed onion, reserved liquid, molasses, syrup, salt, mustard, cinnamon, and ginger. Mix well. Cover and bake 2 hours, stirring occasionally. Add more water to pan if necessary. Uncover and bake 35 to 45 minutes or until top is browned.

Yield: about 8 servings

GINGER CUSTARD

- 5 cups torn white bread pieces
- 2 cups buttermilk
- 2 cups half and half
- 6 apples, peeled, cored, and chopped
- ½ cup water
- ½ cup maple syrup
- ½ cup granulated sugar
- 4 eggs, lightly beaten
- 1 teaspoon ground ginger
- 1 teaspoon ground cinnamon
- 1 teaspoon ground nutmeg
- ¼ teaspoon ground cloves
- 1 cup golden raisins

In a large mixing bowl, combine bread, buttermilk, and half and half; set aside. In a saucepan, combine apples and water over medium heat. Cover and cook until apples are tender; cool.

Preheat oven to 350 degrees. Stir syrup, sugar, eggs, and spices into bread mixture. Stir in apples. Pour mixture into a greased 13 x 9 x 2-inch baking pan. Sprinkle top with raisins. Bake 50 to 60 minutes or until center is set.

Yield: 8 to 10 servings

Featuring layers of tasty plums and egg custard on a pastry crust, Plum Custard is a dessert your family will love. We garnished ours with a maple leaf made of barley sugar.

117

HOLIDAY SWEETS

Adding a sparkle to the joyous spirit of the season, homemade goodies are as much a part of the Christmas celebration as Santa Claus. It seems that during the holidays more than any other time of the year, sumptuous cakes and pies set the stage for laughter and merry-making. As if by magic, trays of warm cookies and creamy candies sweeten the atmosphere. We offer this selection of luscious treats to grace your season's gatherings with gaiety and good taste.

Our Caramel Soufflé has a chewy upper crust, a fluffy filling, and a lining of caramelized sugar that liquefies during baking. Drizzled with Crème Anglaise, it's the next best thing to heaven!

Cranberry Tarts with Orange and Port are a wonderful blend of tangy, spirited flavors. The pecan crust adds a pleasing, nutty taste and texture.

CARAMEL SOUFFLÉ WITH CRÈME ANGLAISE

Because it has a meringue base, this soufflé is amazingly stable and can actually sit at room temperature for several hours before serving.

SOUFFLÉ
2½ cups granulated sugar, divided
8 egg whites
½ teaspoon cream of tartar
⅛ teaspoon salt

CRÈME ANGLAISE
1 cup whipping cream
3 egg yolks, lightly beaten
¼ cup granulated sugar
1 teaspoon vanilla extract

Preheat oven to 300 degrees. For soufflé, place 1¼ cups sugar in a skillet over medium-low heat. Cook, stirring occasionally, until sugar liquefies and turns caramel color (about 5 minutes). Pour half of the caramel into a 2-quart soufflé dish. Tilt dish to coat bottom and sides with caramel; cool. Beat egg whites with cream of tartar and salt until soft peaks form. Gradually beat in remaining 1¼ cups sugar until stiff peaks form. Return skillet to medium-low heat to re-melt remaining caramel. Gradually beat caramel into egg whites; beat 5 minutes. Pour mixture into soufflé dish. Set soufflé dish in a larger baking pan and add water to larger pan to come halfway up the sides of the soufflé dish. Bake 1 hour or until top is firm. (Soufflé may be served warm or at room temperature without falling.)

For Crème Anglaise, heat cream in a heavy saucepan just until cream begins to steam. Whisk about ¼ cup of cream into yolks. Whisk yolk mixture, sugar, and vanilla into remaining cream in saucepan. Return to heat and cook, stirring constantly, until mixture thickens (about 3 to 5 minutes). Remove from heat and strain sauce. Cool completely. Serve with soufflé.
Yield: 8 to 10 servings

CRANBERRY TARTS WITH ORANGE AND PORT

Make the crust and filling for these tarts ahead of time and simply fill the shells before serving. The filling refrigerates well and the shells may be stored in an airtight container two to three days.

CRUST
¾ cup ground toasted pecans
⅓ cup granulated sugar
1½ cups all-purpose flour
½ cup butter, chilled and cut into pieces
3 tablespoons ice water

FILLING
2 cups granulated sugar
4 cups fresh cranberries
1 cup port wine
1 cup water
2 tablespoons orange juice concentrate
1 teaspoon grated orange peel

Sweetened whipped cream to serve (recipe on page 123)

For crust, combine pecans, sugar, and flour in a mixing bowl. Using a pastry blender or two knives, cut butter into pecan mixture until mixture resembles coarse meal. Sprinkle water over dough, mixing quickly just until dough forms a ball. Wrap dough in plastic wrap and refrigerate 1 hour.

Preheat oven to 400 degrees. On a lightly floured surface, use a floured rolling pin to roll out dough to ⅛-inch thickness. Cut the dough into six 5½-inch circles. Place circles of dough in six 4½-inch round tart pans with removable bottoms. Trim edges of dough and prick bottoms of crusts with a fork. Place pans on a baking sheet and bake 12 to 15 minutes or until crusts are lightly browned. Cool completely before filling.

For filling, combine all ingredients in a large saucepan. Bring to a boil over medium-high heat. Reduce heat to simmer and cook, stirring occasionally, until mixture thickens (about 10 minutes). Cool completely.

Just before serving, fill tart shells with cranberry filling. Top with sweetened whipped cream.
Yield: 6 tarts

FRUITCAKE SCONES WITH DEVON CREAM

SCONES
- ¼ cup butter or margarine, softened
- ½ cup granulated sugar
- 2 eggs
- 1½ cups all-purpose flour
- 1½ teaspoons baking powder
- ½ teaspoon baking soda
- ⅛ teaspoon salt
- ½ cup ricotta cheese
- 1 cup dried mixed fruit bits
- ½ cup coarsely chopped pecans
- ¼ cup water
- 1 teaspoon vanilla extract
- 1 teaspoon grated orange peel
- 2 tablespoons brandy

DEVON CREAM
- 1 cup whipping cream, divided
- ¼ cup butter
- 1 tablespoon honey
- ½ teaspoon vanilla extract

Preheat oven to 350 degrees. For scones, cream butter and sugar in a large mixing bowl. Beat in eggs one at a time, beating well after each addition. In a separate bowl, combine flour, baking powder, baking soda, and salt. Stir dry ingredients into butter mixture alternately with ricotta. Stir in fruit, pecans, water, vanilla, and orange peel. Drop about ⅓ cup of dough for each scone onto a lightly greased baking sheet. Bake 12 to 15 minutes until tops are golden brown and a toothpick inserted into a scone comes out clean. Sprinkle warm scones with brandy. Serve scones warm or at room temperature.

For Devon Cream, combine ¼ cup cream and butter in a small saucepan. Place pan over low heat, stirring constantly until butter is melted. Remove pan from heat and stir in honey and vanilla; cool to room temperature.

In a mixing bowl, beat remaining cream until soft peaks form. Gradually beat in butter mixture. Beat 5 minutes at high speed of electric mixer (mixture will appear to be thin). Refrigerate 3 hours. Skim thickened cream off top of mixture and place in serving bowl. Discard any liquid cream at bottom of bowl. Serve with scones. (Devon cream may separate slightly at room temperature, but stirring will correct this. Devon cream will keep in refrigerator 24 hours.)
Yield: 8 scones

CHOCOLATE PATÉ

This chocolate paté with a hint of orange is extra rich and creamy. It may be made up to one week in advance.

- 1 pound semisweet chocolate
- ½ cup Grand Marnier liqueur
- 1¼ cups butter, cut into pieces
- 8 eggs, separated
- ¼ teaspoon salt

Purchased tubes of red and green decorating icing (optional)
Sweetened whipped cream to serve (recipe on page 123)

In the top of a double boiler over low heat, combine chocolate, liqueur, and butter. Stir occasionally until chocolate and butter are melted. Transfer mixture to a large bowl. In a separate bowl, beat egg yolks until pale colored and thick. Fold yolks into chocolate mixture. Chill 1 hour.

In a large bowl, beat egg whites and salt until stiff peaks form. Fold egg whites into chocolate mixture. Pour mixture into a plastic wrap-lined 9 x 5 x 3-inch loaf pan. Cover top and freeze overnight. Remove from pan and use decorating icing to pipe holly onto paté, if desired. Using a knife dipped in hot water, cut into thin slices. Serve with sweetened whipped cream.
Yield: 10 to 12 servings

CHESTNUT POUND CAKE

Look for canned chestnut purée at gourmet groceries.

- 2¾ cups all-purpose flour
- 2 cups granulated sugar
- 2 teaspoons baking soda
- ½ teaspoon salt
- 3 eggs
- ½ cup vegetable oil
- 1 can (15.5 ounces) sweetened chestnut purée
- 1 teaspoon almond extract
- ¾ cup brandy, divided
- 2 cups semisweet chocolate chips

Preheat oven to 350 degrees. In a large mixing bowl, combine flour, sugar, baking soda, and salt, stirring well. Combine eggs and oil and beat into flour mixture. Add chestnut purée, almond extract, and ½ cup brandy, beating until well blended. Stir in chocolate chips. Pour batter into a greased and floured 8-inch springform pan. Bake 1 hour and 15 minutes or until toothpick inserted in center comes out clean. Remove cake from oven and pour remaining ¼ cup brandy over warm cake in pan. Allow cake to cool in pan 1 hour before removing.
Yield: 10 to 12 servings

For an alternative to old-fashioned fruitcake, try sweet, biscuit-like Fruitcake Scones with Devon Cream. They're filled with dried fruit bits and crunchy pecans.

PEAR AND CHOCOLATE TRIFLE

24 ladyfingers
½ cup raspberry jam
 1 can (29 ounces) pear halves, drained
 2 packages (4 ounces each) milk chocolate-flavored instant pudding mix
 2 cups half and half
 1 cup whipping cream
¼ cup granulated sugar
 1 bar (4 ounces) semisweet chocolate, shaved

Split ladyfingers and spread bottoms with jam. Line a trifle or serving bowl with ladyfingers, alternating sides with jam. Line bottom of bowl with ladyfingers, jam side up. Place pears on ladyfingers in bottom of bowl. Beat pudding mix with half and half until thickened. Pour into bowl. Whip cream with sugar until stiff peaks form. Spoon on top of chocolate mixture. Top with shaved chocolate. Cover loosely and refrigerate until ready to serve.
Yield: about 8 servings

Indulge your guests with these rich confections: (*clockwise from top left*) Pear and Chocolate Trifle is an elegant, easy treat. A hint of orange awakens creamy Chocolate Paté. A sprinkling of sugar tops our velvety Chocolate Cream Cake. The Chestnut Pound Cake is laced with brandy and chocolate chips.

CHOCOLATE CREAM CAKE

CAKE
 ½ cup butter or margarine, softened
 4 ounces cream cheese, softened
 2 cups granulated sugar
 2 eggs, lightly beaten
 2 teaspoons vanilla extract
 2 cups all-purpose flour
 ¾ cup cocoa
1½ teaspoons baking soda
 ½ teaspoon salt
 1 cup boiling water

FROSTING
 2 cups semisweet chocolate chips, melted and cooled to room temperature
1½ cups sour cream
 1 teaspoon vanilla extract

Confectioners sugar (optional)

Preheat oven to 350 degrees. For cake, beat butter, cream cheese, and sugar in a large mixing bowl until fluffy. Beat in eggs and vanilla. In a separate bowl, combine flour, cocoa, baking soda, and salt. Blend flour mixture into butter mixture. Stir in water. Pour batter into two greased and floured 9-inch round pans. Bake 25 to 30 minutes or until a toothpick inserted in center of cake comes out clean. Remove cakes from pans and cool on wire racks.

For frosting, beat chocolate, sour cream, and vanilla together until smooth. Frost cake. If decorated top is desired, cut shapes out of paper and place on top of cake. Sift confectioners sugar over top of cake and carefully lift off paper.
Yield: 10 to 12 servings

PEANUT BUTTER FUDGE PIE

CRUST
- 1¼ cups all-purpose flour
- ¼ teaspoon salt
- 7 tablespoons butter, chilled and cut into pieces
- 3 tablespoons ice water

FILLING
- 4 ounces semisweet chocolate
- 3 tablespoons butter or margarine
- ⅓ cup peanut butter
- 1½ teaspoons vanilla extract
- ½ cup plus 2 tablespoons granulated sugar
- 3 eggs
- 1 cup dark corn syrup
- ½ cup milk
- ⅔ cup coarsely chopped roasted unsalted peanuts
- 4 ounces semisweet chocolate bar, broken into small pieces
- 3 tablespoons peanut butter

Preheat oven to 325 degrees. For crust, sift flour and salt into a mixing bowl. Using a pastry blender or two knives, cut butter into flour until mixture resembles coarse meal. Sprinkle ice water over dough, mixing quickly just until dough forms a soft ball. On a lightly floured surface, use a floured rolling pin to roll out dough to ⅛-inch thickness. Place the dough in an ungreased 9-inch pie pan. Trim and crimp edges of dough.

For filling, melt chocolate with butter in the top of a double boiler over low heat. In a large mixing bowl, beat ⅓ cup peanut butter, vanilla, sugar, and eggs until fluffy. Combine corn syrup and milk and gradually beat into the peanut butter mixture. Stir in melted chocolate mixture and peanuts. Pour filling into crust and sprinkle broken chocolate over filling. Dot with remaining peanut butter. Bake 50 minutes to 1 hour or just until the filling is set. Cool pie completely and refrigerate at least 2 hours before serving.

Yield: 8 servings

Peanut Butter Fudge Pie will be a hit with kids of all ages! Chocolate chunks and swirls of peanut butter recreate the flavors of a favorite candy.

POTS DE CRÈME

Serve this rich dessert in very small amounts as an elegant but easy finish to a special holiday meal.

POTS DE CRÈME
- 12 ounces semisweet chocolate
- 2 cups whipping cream
- 6 egg yolks
- 2 tablespoons granulated sugar

SWEETENED WHIPPED CREAM
- 1 cup whipping cream
- ¼ cup granulated sugar
- 1 teaspoon vanilla extract

Preheat oven to 350 degrees. In the top of a double boiler over low heat, melt chocolate with cream, stirring occasionally. In a large bowl, beat egg yolks with sugar. Gradually beat one-fourth of chocolate mixture into egg mixture until well blended. Beat in remaining chocolate mixture. Pour into small custard or demitasse cups to within ½-inch of tops. Place cups in a baking pan and fill pan with hot water to come halfway up the sides of the cups. Bake 30 minutes or until set around edges but still soft in centers; cool. Cover and refrigerate overnight.

For sweetened whipped cream, beat all ingredients until stiff peaks form. Serve with Pots de Crème.
Yield: about 6 Pots de Crème

Chocolate lovers will rejoice in the creamy delights of Pots de Crème, a dense chocolate dessert topped with sweetened whipped cream.

PEPPERMINT STOCKINGS

Old-fashioned, crispy cookies look like stockings hung for Santa. Paste food coloring will give good intensity of color without diluting the icing.

COOKIES
- 3¼ cups all-purpose flour
- 1 tablespoon baking powder
- ½ cup butter or margarine, softened
- 1¼ cups granulated sugar
- 1 egg
- 2½ teaspoons peppermint extract
- 1 teaspoon vanilla extract
- ¼ cup milk

ICING
- 1 cup confectioners sugar
- 1 tablespoon butter, softened
- 2 tablespoons milk
  Red paste food coloring

Preheat oven to 350 degrees. In a medium mixing bowl, combine flour and baking powder. In a large mixing bowl, cream butter, sugar, egg, and extracts. Add the dry ingredients alternately with milk. On a lightly floured surface, use a floured rolling pin to roll out dough to ⅛-inch thickness. Using desired cookie cutter, cut out dough. Transfer cookies to a lightly greased baking sheet. Bake 8 to 10 minutes or until very lightly browned around edges. Remove from pans and cool on wire racks.

For icing, beat together sugar, butter, and milk until smooth. Stir in food coloring. Ice cookies as desired.
Yield: about 3 dozen 3-inch long cookies

Surprise Santa with these whimsical Peppermint Stockings. He'll love them — and so will the kids!

GINGERBREAD TOASTS

Lighter in color than most gingerbread, these cookies get extra zing from crystallized ginger. Try them with a cup of tea.

2½ cups all-purpose flour
3 teaspoons baking powder
¾ teaspoon salt
¼ cup finely minced crystallized ginger
½ teaspoon ground ginger
¼ teaspoon ground cinnamon
½ cup butter or margarine, softened
¾ cup granulated sugar
1 teaspoon vanilla extract
2 eggs
⅔ cup blanched whole almonds, toasted and coarsely chopped
2 teaspoons milk
Granulated sugar

Preheat oven to 375 degrees. Combine flour, baking powder, salt, crystallized ginger, ground ginger, and cinnamon. In a separate mixing bowl, beat butter and sugar until fluffy. Beat in vanilla and eggs. Stir in the flour mixture and almonds. Divide the dough in half and mold each half into a 12 x 2-inch strip on a foil-lined baking sheet. Smooth the surface of each strip. Brush each with milk; then sprinkle with sugar. Bake 18 to 20 minutes or until light golden brown and firm to the touch. Remove from oven and reduce temperature to 300 degrees. Place the strips on a wire rack and cool 15 minutes.

Place the strips on a cutting board and use a serrated knife to cut each strip crosswise on the diagonal into ½-inch thick slices. Place the slices on the baking sheet and bake 10 minutes. Turn the slices over and bake 10 minutes more. Turn off the heat and allow the toasts to cool in the oven, leaving the door slightly ajar.
Yield: about 3 dozen toasts

CARAMEL BAKED APPLES

6 tablespoons butter or margarine, softened
2 teaspoons ground nutmeg
6 red baking apples, cored
¼ cup plus 2 tablespoons water, divided
1 package (10 ounces) caramels
½ cup whipping cream

Sweetened whipped cream to serve (recipe on page 123)

Preheat oven to 350 degrees. In a small bowl, combine butter and nutmeg. Using 1 tablespoon for each apple, fill centers of apples with butter mixture. Place apples in a baking pan and add ¼ cup water to bottom of pan. Bake 30 to 35 minutes.

In a heavy saucepan over low heat, melt caramels with 2 tablespoons water, stirring occasionally. Remove from heat and stir in cream. To serve, pour caramel mixture over baked apples. Serve with sweetened whipped cream.
Yield: 6 apples

Chock-full of almonds and zippy crystallized ginger, crunchy Gingerbread Toasts are light, flavorful sweets.

Melted caramel and a hint of nutmeg add a sweet touch to an old favorite. Crowned with dollops of whipped cream, Caramel Baked Apples are sure to please!

Packed with pecans, chewy Date Muffins are moist, spicy treats. Top them with a hard sauce and gumdrop holly berries for a delectable difference.

DATE MUFFINS

MUFFINS
- 1 package (8 ounces) chopped dates
- 1 cup granulated sugar
- 3 eggs, beaten
- ½ cup all-purpose flour
- ½ teaspoon salt
- ½ teaspoon ground cinnamon
- ¼ teaspoon ground nutmeg
- 1¼ cups chopped toasted pecans

HARD SAUCE
- 2 cups confectioners sugar
- ½ cup butter, softened
- 1 teaspoon vanilla extract

Preheat oven to 350 degrees. For muffins, combine all ingredients in a large mixing bowl. Stir just until all ingredients are moistened. Fill lightly greased miniature muffin tins two-thirds full with batter. Bake 15 minutes or until tops are very lightly browned and a muffin springs back when lightly pressed. Remove from tins and cool on wire racks.

For hard sauce, combine all ingredients in a medium bowl and beat until smooth. Frost tops of muffins with hard sauce.

Yield: about 4 dozen muffins

LEMON CURD TARTS

Pretty gumdrop roses top these tangy lemon tarts. Simply roll half of a red gumdrop between two sheets of waxed paper and roll into a rose shape. Roll out a green gumdrop and use a sharp knife to cut small leaf shapes from it.

CRUST
- 1¼ cups all-purpose flour
- 2 tablespoons granulated sugar
- ¼ teaspoon salt
- ½ cup butter, chilled and cut into pieces
- 3 tablespoons ice water

LEMON CURD
- 6 egg yolks
- 1 cup granulated sugar
- 6 tablespoons butter, cut into pieces
- ½ cup fresh lemon juice
- 1½ tablespoons grated lemon peel
- ⅛ teaspoon salt

Sweetened whipped cream to serve (recipe on page 123)

For crust, sift flour, sugar, and salt into a mixing bowl. Using a pastry blender or two knives, cut butter into flour until mixture resembles coarse meal. Sprinkle ice water over dough, mixing quickly just until dough forms a soft ball. Wrap dough in plastic wrap and refrigerate 1 hour.

Preheat oven to 400 degrees. On a lightly floured surface, use a floured rolling pin to roll out dough to ⅛-inch thickness. Cut out dough in shapes about ¼-inch larger than tartlet pans. Press into pans; trim excess around edges. Refrigerate 30 minutes. Line pans with small pieces of aluminum foil and weight foil with dried beans or pie weights. Bake 10 minutes. Remove weights and foil and bake 3 to 5 minutes more or until very lightly browned. Cool completely before removing tart shells from pans.

For Lemon Curd, combine all ingredients in a heavy, non-aluminum saucepan over medium-low heat. Cook, stirring constantly, until butter is melted and mixture thickens slightly. Do not allow mixture to boil. Remove from heat. Transfer mixture to a bowl and cool. Cover and refrigerate at least 2 hours before serving.

To serve, fill tart shells with Lemon Curd and top with a small amount of sweetened whipped cream.
Yield: about 16 tarts

ORANGE COOKIES WITH CHOCOLATE FILLING

COOKIES
- 1 cup granulated sugar
- 2 eggs
- 1 teaspoon vanilla extract
- 1 cup vegetable shortening
- 3 tablespoons orange juice concentrate
- 2 tablespoons grated orange peel
- 4½ cups all-purpose flour
- 1 teaspoon baking soda
- ½ teaspoon baking powder
- ½ teaspoon salt
- ½ cup buttermilk

FILLING
- 1 cup semisweet chocolate chips, melted
- 2 tablespoons whipping cream
- 2½ teaspoons orange extract

For cookies, cream sugar, eggs, vanilla, shortening, orange juice concentrate, and orange peel in a large mixing bowl. Combine dry ingredients and add to creamed mixture alternately with buttermilk. Divide dough in half and wrap in plastic wrap. Refrigerate at least 2 hours or until well chilled.

Preheat oven to 375 degrees. On a lightly floured surface, use a floured rolling pin to roll out dough to ⅛-inch thickness. Using 2-inch round cookie cutter, cut out dough. Transfer cookies to a lightly greased baking sheet. Bake 6 to 8 minutes or until very lightly browned around edges. Remove from pans and cool on wire racks.

For filling, combine all ingredients, blending until smooth. Spread a thin layer of filling on bottom of one cookie, and place another cookie on top of filling. Allow chocolate to set by placing cookies in the refrigerator 5 minutes.
Yield: about 4 dozen cookies

Share these goodies at party time or anytime: (*clockwise from top left*) A cheese pastry complements the sweet filling in Apple-Cheddar Turnovers. Delicately flavored with almond, the creamy filling of our Ricotta Cream Cornets is sprinkled with chocolate bits. Crispy Orange Cookies with Chocolate Filling are a yummy snack. A layer of marshmallow is nestled beneath the frosting of our Mississippi Mud Brownies. Lemon Curd Tarts are a popular English teatime dessert.

IRISH CREAM DESSERT

- 1 envelope unflavored gelatin
- 3 tablespoons cold water
- 2 cups whipping cream
- ½ cup Irish Cream liqueur
- ½ cup granulated sugar
- ½ cup finely chopped semisweet or bittersweet chocolate, reserving 2 tablespoons for garnish

In a small, heat-proof bowl combine gelatin and water. Allow to sit 5 minutes to soften gelatin. Place bowl in a saucepan of water over low heat and stir until gelatin is dissolved. Remove from heat and cool to room temperature.

In a large mixing bowl, whip cream until soft peaks form. Gradually beat gelatin into cream until stiff peaks form. Blend in liqueur and sugar. Fold in chocolate. Spoon into individual glasses and chill at least 1 hour. Before serving, sprinkle reserved chocolate over tops of desserts.

Yield: about 8 servings

RICOTTA CREAM CORNETS

PASTRY

- 1 sheet frozen puff pastry dough, thawed according to package directions
  Metal cornet molds
- 1 egg white
- 1 teaspoon water

FILLING

- 1 cup ricotta cheese
- ¼ cup confectioners sugar
- 1 teaspoon vanilla extract
- ½ teaspoon almond extract
- ½ cup semisweet miniature chocolate chips

Preheat oven to 350 degrees. Cut dough into strips about ¾ x 10 inches. Beginning at the tip of one of the molds, wrap the strip of dough around the mold without stretching dough. The strip will only cover about three-fourths of the mold. Repeat with remaining strips and molds.

Combine the egg white with water. Brush over dough. Place the molds on a baking sheet. Bake 20 minutes or until golden. Carefully remove the pastry from the molds and cool on a wire rack.

For filling, beat ricotta, confectioners sugar, and extracts in a medium mixing bowl until smooth. Stir in chocolate chips. Just before serving, use a pastry bag or spoon to fill pastries with filling.

Yield: 8 to 10 cornets

MISSISSIPPI MUD BROWNIES

BROWNIES

- 1 package (19.8 ounces) fudge brownie mix
- ½ cup water
- ⅓ cup vegetable oil
- 1 egg
- ¼ cup all-purpose flour
- 1½ cups miniature marshmallows

FROSTING

- ½ cup semisweet chocolate chips, melted
- ⅓ cup milk
- 2 tablespoons butter or margarine
- 1¾ cups confectioners sugar

  Purchased tubes of red and green decorating icing (optional)

Preheat oven to 350 degrees. In a medium mixing bowl, combine brownie mix, water, oil, egg, and flour, stirring just until blended. Pour batter into a lightly greased 10 x 8 x 2-inch baking pan. Bake 25 to 30 minutes or until center is set. Top with marshmallows and bake 2 minutes longer.

For frosting, combine melted chocolate, milk, butter, and sugar. Beat until smooth and spread over brownies. Cut into bars.

If desired, use decorating icing to pipe small red and green bows on tops of brownies.

Yield: about 20 brownies

Light and fluffy, this sumptuous Irish Cream Dessert is kissed with the flavor of a favorite liqueur. It's a cool way to warm up on a frosty night.

APPLE-CHEDDAR TURNOVERS

CRUST

- 1⅓ cups all-purpose flour
- ½ teaspoon salt
- ½ cup butter, chilled and cut into pieces
- ½ cup finely grated mild Cheddar cheese
- 2 tablespoons ice water
- 1 egg yolk
- 1 teaspoon water

FILLING

- 2 apples, peeled, cored, and chopped
- 6 tablespoons butter or margarine
- ⅓ cup firmly packed brown sugar
- 1 tablespoon all-purpose flour
- ½ teaspoon ground cinnamon
- ¼ teaspoon ground cloves
  Butter or margarine

For crust, sift flour and salt into a mixing bowl. Using a pastry blender or two knives, cut butter into flour until mixture resembles coarse meal. Stir in cheese. Sprinkle ice water over dough, mixing quickly just until dough forms a soft ball. Wrap dough in plastic wrap and refrigerate 1 hour.

For filling, sauté apples in butter over medium heat, stirring frequently until apples are soft. Stir in brown sugar, flour, and spices and cook, stirring constantly, for 1 minute. Remove from heat and cool completely.

On a lightly floured surface, use a floured rolling pin to roll out dough to ⅛-inch thickness. Cut dough into 4-inch circles (we used the ring from a 4-inch pastry pan with removable bottom). Combine egg yolk and water. Brush pastry circles with egg yolk mixture. Place 1 heaping tablespoon of filling in the center of each circle and dot with butter. Fold pastry over filling, pressing edges to seal. Brush outside of pastry with egg yolk mixture. Cut slits in tops of turnovers for steam to escape. Refrigerate 30 minutes.

Preheat oven to 350 degrees. Bake 20 to 25 minutes or until golden brown.

Yield: about 8 turnovers

PEAR AND ALMOND TART

This elegant tart is quick and easy to make with ingredients that may be kept on your pantry shelf.

CRUST

- 1¼ cups all-purpose flour
- ¼ teaspoon salt
- ⅓ cup granulated sugar
- 7 tablespoons butter, chilled and cut into pieces
- 3 tablespoons ice water

FILLING

- ½ cup butter or margarine, softened
- 1 cup almond paste
- 2 eggs
- 1 teaspoon vanilla extract
- 1 can (29 ounces) pear halves, drained
- 1 tablespoon granulated sugar
- 3 tablespoons peach preserves

CHOCOLATE SPLURGE

Crispy cookie bits give this smooth dessert extra crunch. This dessert may be frozen for up to one week — if it lasts that long!

- ½ cup butter or margarine, softened
- ¾ cup confectioners sugar
- 1 egg
- ½ cup cocoa
- 3 ounces semisweet chocolate, melted
- 2 tablespoons crème de menthe liqueur
- 4 cups (about 14 ounces) chocolate mint-flavored cookies, broken into small pieces

  Sweetened whipped cream to serve (recipe on page 123)

In a medium mixing bowl, beat butter, sugar, and egg until creamy. Blend in cocoa, chocolate, and liqueur. Stir in cookies. Turn mixture into a plastic wrap-lined 8-inch round pan. Cover and chill until firm (1 to 2 hours). Serve with sweetened whipped cream.
Yield: 8 to 10 servings

Preheat oven to 350 degrees. For crust, sift flour, salt, and sugar together in a medium mixing bowl. Using a pastry blender or two knives, cut butter into flour until mixture resembles coarse meal. Sprinkle ice water over dough, mixing quickly just until dough forms a soft ball. On a lightly floured surface, use a floured rolling pin to roll out dough to ⅛-inch thickness. Place the dough in an ungreased 10½-inch tart pan with removable bottom. Trim edges of dough.

For filling, beat butter and almond paste in a medium mixing bowl until fluffy. Beat in the eggs one at a time, beating well after each addition. Beat in vanilla. Spread filling in shell. Arrange pear halves over the filling. Bake 40 minutes or until filling is golden and set. Sprinkle tart with sugar and broil until bubbly and browned (watch closely, this happens very quickly). Brush with preserves while tart is still warm. Cool completely before cutting.
Yield: 10 to 12 servings

This trio of elegant desserts is ideal for special occasions: (*clockwise from top left*) A sweet almond flavor highlights the delightfully simple European-style Pear and Almond Tart. Chocolate Splurge is smooth and crunchy; chocolate mint cookies and crème de menthe liqueur add extra coolness to this frozen delight. Rich Vanilla Pastries with Cherry Sauce make a luscious ending to a holiday party.

For an elegant holiday dessert, serve Amaretto Truffles in a glass with liqueur and whipped cream. They also make a wonderful after-dinner candy.

AMARETTO TRUFFLES

Keep a tin of these truffles in your refrigerator as a special treat to serve drop-in guests. Whether you serve them in a glass with liqueur and cream or as a candy, they are sure to be a hit.

- 2 cups semisweet chocolate chips
- ½ cup butter or margarine, softened
- 2 egg yolks
- 3 tablespoons cream cheese
- ⅓ cup amaretto liqueur
- 1 cup finely chopped toasted almonds

  Amaretto liqueur to serve (optional)
  Sweetened whipped cream to serve (optional, recipe on page 123)

Melt chocolate chips in the top of a double boiler over low heat. Remove from heat and stir in butter one tablespoon at a time. Beat egg yolks into mixture (mixture will begin to thicken). Beat cream cheese and ⅓ cup amaretto into chocolate mixture until smooth. Cover and chill until firm.

Shape mixture into 1½-inch balls. Roll in almonds. Refrigerate until firm. To serve, pour about 2 tablespoons amaretto into a wine glass. Place a truffle in glass and top with whipped cream.

Yield: about 36 truffles

VANILLA PASTRIES WITH CHERRY SAUCE

PASTRY
- 1 sheet frozen puff pastry dough, thawed according to package directions
- 1 egg yolk
- 1 teaspoon water
- 1 tablespoon granulated sugar

CUSTARD
- 1 cup plus 2 tablespoons milk, divided
- 2 eggs, separated
- ¼ cup cornstarch
- 2 tablespoons granulated sugar
- 2 teaspoons vanilla extract
- ¾ cup confectioners sugar

ICING
- 1 cup confectioners sugar
- 3 tablespoons lemon juice

CHERRY SAUCE
- 1 can (16½ ounces) pitted dark sweet cherries, drained
- ⅓ cup firmly packed brown sugar
- 2 tablespoons lemon juice

Preheat oven to 400 degrees. For pastry, cut puff pastry sheet in half lengthwise. Place pastry halves on a lightly greased baking sheet and prick each half several times with a fork. Combine egg yolk with water and brush over pastry halves. Sprinkle each half with sugar. Bake 15 to 20 minutes or until golden brown. Cool completely before removing from pan.

For custard, combine 2 tablespoons milk, egg yolks, cornstarch, sugar, and vanilla in a mixing bowl, blending well. In a large heavy saucepan, bring 1 cup milk to a boil. Whisk about half of hot milk into egg mixture. Whisk egg mixture into remaining milk in pan. Cook over medium heat, stirring constantly until mixture is very thick (about 2 to 3 minutes). Remove from heat. In a large mixing bowl, beat egg whites with confectioners sugar until stiff and shiny. Fold egg white mixture into warm mixture in pan. Cool completely, cover, and refrigerate 1 hour.

For icing, combine confectioners sugar and lemon juice in a small bowl, blending until smooth.

Spread custard thickly over one pastry half. Top with remaining pastry half and spread icing over top. Chill at least 1 hour. Use a serrated knife to cut pastry into slices.

For cherry sauce, purée cherries with brown sugar and lemon juice in a blender or food processor. Allow to stand at room temperature 15 minutes. To serve, place a spoonful of sauce on a dessert plate and top with a pastry slice.

Yield: about 8 pastries

WHITE CHOCOLATE CHEESECAKE

To make the leaves that top this dessert, stir 2 tablespoons light corn syrup into 6 ounces of melted green candy coating wafers. Wrap in plastic wrap and let set overnight at room temperature. Knead mixture and roll out between two sheets of waxed paper. Cut out leaves with a cookie cutter. Whole cranberries complete the garnish.

CHEESECAKE
- 2 packages (8 ounces each) cream cheese, softened
- ⅓ cup granulated sugar
- 6 egg yolks
- 1 tablespoon vanilla extract
- ½ teaspoon salt
- 2 cups sour cream
- 12 ounces white chocolate, melted

FROSTING
- 1 package (8 ounces) cream cheese, softened
- ⅓ cup butter, softened
- 1 teaspoon vanilla extract
- 8 ounces white chocolate, melted

Preheat oven to 350 degrees. For cheesecake, beat cream cheese and sugar in a large mixing bowl until smooth. Beat in egg yolks one at a time, beating well after each addition. Beat in vanilla, salt, and sour cream. Blend in white chocolate. Pour the batter into a lightly greased 8-inch springform pan. Place springform pan in a larger pan and add water to larger pan to come halfway up side of springform pan. Bake 45 minutes. Turn off the oven and allow the cake to cool in the oven 1 hour without opening the door. Remove cheesecake from oven and pan of water and allow to cool completely. Cover and refrigerate overnight.

For frosting, beat cream cheese, butter, and vanilla in a medium mixing bowl until smooth. Gradually beat in white chocolate. Use a knife to loosen sides of cheesecake from pan; remove springform. Spread frosting over top and sides of cheesecake. Chill at least 1 hour before serving.
Yield: 10 to 12 servings

Covered with a luscious white chocolate buttercream frosting, this rich White Chocolate Cheesecake can be made ahead of time and frozen for up to a week.

130

MARSHMALLOW-MINT SANDWICHES

- 2 packages (12½ ounces each) fudge-covered graham crackers
- 1 cup water, divided
- 2 envelopes unflavored gelatin
- 2¼ cups granulated sugar
- 1½ teaspoons peppermint extract
- 1 teaspoon vanilla extract
  Red food coloring

- 1 ounce vanilla-flavored candy coating

Line the bottom of an ungreased 13 x 9 x 2-inch baking pan with 36 graham crackers, top sides down.
In a large mixing bowl, combine ½ cup water and gelatin; set aside. In a saucepan, combine remaining ½ cup water and sugar. Bring to a boil and boil 2 minutes. Stir sugar mixture into gelatin, blending well. Refrigerate 10 minutes. Beat at highest speed of electric mixer until mixture turns white and becomes thick like meringue. Beat in extracts and a few drops of food coloring. Pour mixture over crackers. Top mixture with 36 crackers, top sides up. Refrigerate until set, about 1 hour. Using a sharp knife dipped in hot water, cut into sandwiches using cookie tops as guidelines.
If desired, melt candy coating and add a drop of food coloring to tint a pale pink. Drizzle candy coating over tops of cookies. Store at room temperature.
Yield: 36 cookies

Pink and pretty, Marshmallow-Mint Sandwiches are quick-and-easy treats that children will love.

Cinnamon, ginger, and cloves add spice to the mellow goodness of Pumpkin Ice Cream.

PUMPKIN ICE CREAM

With the popularity and ease of today's ice cream makers, it's possible to make this frozen treat year-round!

2 cups whipping cream
2 cups milk
1 cup granulated sugar
4 egg yolks, lightly beaten
1 cup canned pumpkin
1 teaspoon ground cinnamon
½ teaspoon ground ginger
¼ teaspoon ground cloves

In a heavy saucepan, combine cream, milk, and sugar over medium heat. Cook just until mixture begins to steam and remove from heat. Whisk about ¼ cup of cream mixture into egg yolks. Whisk yolk mixture into cream mixture in pan. Return to heat and cook, stirring constantly until mixture coats the back of a metal spoon. Remove from heat and cool completely. Stir in remaining ingredients. Pour into an ice cream maker and freeze following manufacturer's instructions.
Yield: about 5½ cups of ice cream

CHRISTMAS TIDBITS

As we invite friends and loved ones into our homes during the holidays, we delight in making them welcome. The warmth of friendship and Christmas spirit bind us together in celebration of the season as we share delicious homemade treats. Whether your holiday get-together is a big open house or a small intimate gathering, our sampling of delicious snacks and appetizers will help you create a joyous atmosphere of hospitality.

Creamy, garlic-flavored Aioli Dip is delightful with fresh vegetables, seafood, or French bread.

chocolate pecan pie

Yield: 1 (9-inch) pie

½ (14.1-ounce) package refrigerated piecrusts
1½ cups pecan halves
1 (4-ounce) bar bittersweet chocolate, finely chopped
3 large eggs
¾ cup dark corn syrup
⅔ cup sugar
¼ cup firmly packed dark brown sugar
5 tablespoons butter, melted and slightly cooled
1 tablespoon all-purpose flour
1 teaspoon vanilla extract
½ teaspoon salt

1. Preheat oven to 350°. Unroll piecrust on a lightly floured surface. Roll into a 12-inch circle; fit dough into a 9-inch pie plate. Fold edges under and flute as desired. Sprinkle pecans and chocolate in bottom of prepared crust.

2. In a large bowl, place eggs; whisk until foamy. Add corn syrup, sugars, melted butter, flour, vanilla, and salt; whisk until thoroughly combined. Pour over pecan mixture.

3. Bake until crust is golden brown and filling is set, 45 to 50 minutes. Let cool completely on a wire rack before serving.

cover recipe

Succulent Chinese Chicken Wings are basted with a mixture of soy sauce, horseradish, and plum jam. Cheddar cheese, strawberry jam, bacon, and pecans give Cheese Pockets a sensational taste.

AIOLI DIP

   3 garlic cloves, minced
   2 egg yolks, beaten
 ¼ teaspoon salt
 ⅛ teaspoon white pepper
 ¼ cup lemon juice
   1 teaspoon Dijon-style mustard
 ⅛ teaspoon cayenne pepper
1½ cups olive oil

     See serving suggestions below

In a food processor or blender, purée garlic. Add egg yolks, salt, pepper, lemon juice, mustard, and cayenne. Process until smooth. With the motor running, pour the oil very slowly into the mixture in a steady stream. Continue processing until mixture becomes thick and firm. Chill until ready to serve. Serve with artichoke hearts, hearts of palm, blanched snow peas, carrots, cauliflower, strips of bell pepper, cherry tomatoes, zucchini, hard-cooked eggs, chunks of cooked lobster, cooked shrimp, or chunks of French bread.
Yield: about 2 cups of dip

CHEESE POCKETS

   1 package (10 ounces) refrigerated prepared pizza dough
 ¼ cup strawberry jam
 ¾ cup grated sharp Cheddar cheese
 ¼ cup chopped green onion
   5 slices bacon, cooked and crumbled
 ¼ cup chopped pecans

Preheat oven to 400 degrees. Unroll pizza dough and cut into 12 equal pieces. Place one teaspoon jam on each piece of dough. Top with cheese, green onion, bacon, and pecans. Brush edges of dough with water. Fold dough over filling and seal edges with fork. Place pockets on a lightly greased baking sheet. Bake 12 to 15 minutes or until golden brown. Serve warm.
Yield: 12 pockets

CHINESE CHICKEN WINGS

1½ pounds chicken wings, disjointed and wingtips discarded
 ½ cup red plum jam
   3 tablespoons soy sauce
   3 to 4 drops hot pepper sauce
   2 tablespoons prepared horseradish
   1 tablespoon prepared mustard

     Chinese hot mustard to serve

Preheat oven to 425 degrees. Place wings in a single layer on a baking sheet. Combine remaining ingredients and brush generously over wings. Bake 15 to 20 minutes, basting frequently. Serve with Chinese hot mustard, if desired.
Yield: about 20 chicken wings

MINI HOT BROWNS

 3 tablespoons butter or margarine
 3 tablespoons all-purpose flour
 ½ cup grated sharp Cheddar cheese
 1 cup milk
 ½ teaspoon salt
 ½ teaspoon white pepper
 1½ cups finely diced cooked turkey
   breast
 8 slices bacon, cooked and
   crumbled
 20 slices thinly sliced white bread
 ¾ cup freshly grated Parmesan
   cheese

In a medium saucepan, melt butter over medium-low heat. Stir in flour, blending well. Add Cheddar cheese, stirring constantly until smooth. Increase heat to medium and slowly stir in milk, whisking constantly. Cook 4 to 5 minutes, stirring constantly, until the sauce is thick and smooth. Remove from heat and stir in salt, pepper, turkey, and bacon; set aside.

Preheat broiler. Trim crusts from bread and cut each slice into four squares. Place bread on baking sheets and toast on one side under broiler.

Spread a heaping tablespoon of turkey mixture on untoasted side of each piece of bread. Place on baking sheets. Sprinkle with Parmesan cheese. Broil a few seconds or until Parmesan melts and mixture begins to bubble.
Yield: 80 appetizers

The fresh-baked goodness of Soft Breadsticks is enhanced by smoky Madeira Cheese Spread.

SOFT BREADSTICKS

 1 package active dry yeast
 1½ cups warm water
 2 tablespoons granulated sugar
 1¼ teaspoons salt
 4½ cups all-purpose flour
 1 egg
 1 tablespoon water
   Coarse salt or margarita salt

In a large mixing bowl, combine yeast, 1½ cups warm water, sugar, and 1¼ teaspoons salt. Stir to dissolve and allow to sit 5 minutes. Gradually stir in flour, blending well to make a smooth dough. Turn out dough on a lightly floured surface and knead until smooth and elastic, 8 to 10 minutes. Divide dough into 28 equal pieces. Roll each piece into an approximately 8 x ¼-inch breadstick. Place on a greased baking sheet.

In a small bowl, combine egg with 1 tablespoon water. Brush mixture over breadsticks and sprinkle with coarse salt. Cover and let rise 25 minutes.

Preheat oven to 425 degrees. Bake 15 to 20 minutes or until brown. Remove from pan and cool on wire rack.
Yield: 28 breadsticks

MADEIRA CHEESE SPREAD

 ½ cup Madeira wine
 ⅓ cup butter, melted
 14 ounces Gouda cheese
 1 cup sour cream
 1 teaspoon salt
 ⅛ teaspoon cayenne pepper

In a small bowl, combine wine and butter. In a food processor or blender, combine cheese, sour cream, salt, and cayenne. Process until smooth. With motor running, gradually add wine mixture, blending until smooth. Refrigerate 24 hours before serving to allow flavors to blend.
Yield: about 2½ cups of spread

These cheesy appetizers will delight guests: (clockwise from top) Greek Potato Skins, Mini Hot Browns, and Ham Pinwheels.

CORNMEAL CHICKEN NUGGETS

½ cup cornmeal
1 tablespoon chili powder
2 teaspoons ground cumin
4 boneless, skinless chicken breasts, cut into 1-inch cubes
3 tablespoons vegetable oil

Combine cornmeal, chili powder, and cumin; mix well. Add chicken and toss to coat well with mixture. In a large skillet, heat oil over medium heat. Add chicken and cook, stirring frequently 5 to 6 minutes or until chicken is browned on all sides and done in middle. Serve with Adobado Sauce.
Yield: about 36 nuggets

ADOBADO SAUCE

2 cans (4 ounces each) chopped mild chili peppers
1 cup chicken broth
3 tablespoons butter or margarine
2 medium onions, diced
2 tablespoons ground cumin
2 teaspoons chili powder
2 garlic cloves, minced
¼ cup firmly packed light brown sugar
¼ cup orange juice
¼ cup catsup
2 tablespoons lemon juice

In a blender or food processor, purée peppers. Combine chili purée with chicken broth and set aside.

In a large skillet, melt butter over medium heat. Add onions and cook 15 minutes, stirring frequently. Blend in cumin, chili powder, and garlic. Stir in chili purée mixture. Reduce heat to medium-low and cook 20 minutes, stirring frequently.

Combine brown sugar, orange juice, catsup, and lemon juice. Stir into chili mixture. Continue cooking, stirring occasionally, about 15 minutes or until mixture is the consistency of thick purée. Cool slightly. Serve warm or at room temperature.
Yield: about 2¾ cups of sauce

Spicy Cornmeal Chicken Nuggets served with Adobado Sauce bring Southwest flavor to your holiday gathering.

ORANGE CREAM

- 4 cups orange juice
- 3 cinnamon sticks
- 1 tablespoon vanilla extract
- 1 pint vanilla ice cream

Miniature marshmallows to serve

In a large saucepan, combine orange juice, cinnamon sticks, and vanilla over medium-high heat. Bring mixture to a boil and reduce to low heat. Simmer 10 minutes. Remove cinnamon sticks. Stir in ice cream. Cook over low heat, stirring constantly, until heated through. Do not allow mixture to boil. Serve with miniature marshmallows.
Yield: 4 to 6 servings

Luscious Orange Cream, a mixture of orange juice and vanilla ice cream, is flavored with a hint of cinnamon. Serve it warm for a special holiday beverage.

GOUGERE

- ½ cup butter or margarine
- 1¼ cups all-purpose flour
- 4 eggs
- 3 cups grated sharp Cheddar cheese
- 1 cup grated Swiss cheese
- ½ teaspoon salt
- ¼ teaspoon freshly ground pepper
- 1 garlic clove, minced
- 2 jalapeño peppers, chopped
- ¼ cup chopped onion
- ⅛ teaspoon cayenne pepper

Preheat oven to 375 degrees. In a medium saucepan, melt butter over medium heat. Add flour and stir until mixture forms a ball. Remove from heat and continue stirring until mixture cools. Beat in eggs, one at a time, stirring until mixture is slightly glossy and smooth. Stir in remaining ingredients. Pour batter into a greased 10-inch iron skillet. Bake 40 to 45 minutes or until golden brown. Cut bread into slices to serve.
Yield: about 32 slices of bread

Gougere is a hearty bread flavored with Cheddar and Swiss cheeses and hot jalapeño peppers.

SUN-DRIED TOMATO SPREAD

  1 cup sun dried tomatoes
     Boiling water
  2 garlic cloves, minced
  1 tablespoon capers
  2 teaspoons Italian seasoning
  1 teaspoon salt
  5 tablespoons olive oil
  2 tablespoons red wine vinegar

     Melba toast to serve
     Ricotta cheese to serve

Place tomatoes in a small bowl and add boiling water to cover. Let sit 15 minutes; drain.

Place tomatoes in a food processor and purée. Add garlic, capers, Italian seasoning, salt, oil, and vinegar. Process until well blended and mixture is still slightly coarse. Adjust seasonings, if desired. Store in a jar in the refrigerator until ready to serve. To serve, spread melba toast with ricotta cheese and top with sun-dried tomato spread.
Yield: about 1 cup of spread

MINI BAGELS WITH DILLED SHRIMP SPREAD

½ pound cooked shrimp, shelled, deveined, and finely chopped
  2 garlic cloves, minced
  1 package (8 ounces) cream cheese, softened
  2 tablespoons mayonnaise
  2 tablespoons sherry
  1 tablespoon lemon juice
½ teaspoon salt
½ teaspoon lemon pepper
½ teaspoon dillweed

20 mini bagels, split to serve

Combine all ingredients, blending well. Pack into a small bowl. Cover and chill at least 1 hour before serving with mini bagels.
Yield: about 2 cups of spread

Little open-faced sandwiches make great finger foods: Mini Bagels with Dilled Shrimp Spread *(top)* are flavored with dill and garlic. Sun-Dried Tomato Spread is delicious on melba toast with ricotta cheese.

CARNITAS

1 pound bulk pork sausage
½ cup diced onion
½ cup diced bell pepper
3 tablespoons catsup
2 teaspoons chili powder
½ teaspoon cumin
⅛ teaspoon ground cloves
24 miniature taco shells

Grated Cheddar cheese to serve
Shredded lettuce to serve

In a skillet over medium heat, brown sausage with onion and bell pepper; drain well. Stir in catsup, chili powder, cumin, and cloves. Cook 3 minutes, stirring constantly. Drain again. Serve mixture in taco shells with cheese and lettuce.
Yield: 24 miniature tacos

MUSHROOM AND CHICKEN PASTRIES

2 cans (5 ounces each) chunk white chicken, drained and chopped
1 cup finely chopped fresh mushrooms
¼ cup minced onion
1 teaspoon garlic salt
2 tablespoons Worcestershire sauce
⅓ cup mayonnaise
1 teaspoon lemon pepper
½ teaspoon grated lemon peel
2 tablespoons minced fresh parsley
1 package frozen puff pastry dough, thawed according to package directions

Combine all ingredients except puff pastry dough. Blend well, cover, and refrigerate until ready to use.

Preheat oven to 350 degrees. Unfold puff pastry dough. Using a 2-inch round cookie cutter, cut out dough. Place circles on lightly greased baking sheet and bake 15 to 20 minutes or until puffed and golden. Cool slightly and use a sharp knife to cut off tops of pastries; set aside. Remove soft inner dough from pastries. Fill with chicken mixture; replace tops.
Yield: about 40 pastries

MUSHROOM CROUSTADES

36 slices thin wheat bread, cut into 3-inch rounds
¼ cup butter or margarine
⅓ cup finely chopped green onion
8 ounces fresh mushrooms, finely chopped
2 tablespoons all-purpose flour
1 tablespoon minced fresh parsley
½ teaspoon salt
⅛ teaspoon cayenne pepper
1 pound bulk pork sausage, browned and drained
1 cup whipping cream
2 teaspoons lemon juice
3 tablespoons freshly grated Parmesan cheese

Preheat oven to 400 degrees. Carefully fit bread into lightly greased miniature muffin tins, pressing gently into sides to form cups. Bake 8 to 10 minutes or until firm to touch.

In a large skillet, melt butter over medium-high heat. Add green onion and sauté 3 to 4 minutes. Stir in mushrooms and cook, stirring constantly, 10 to 15 minutes or until most of liquid is evaporated. Stir in flour, parsley, salt, and cayenne until well blended. Stir in sausage and cream and bring to a low boil. Reduce heat to medium-low and simmer until mixture thickens, about 10 minutes. Stir in lemon juice and remove from heat. Let cool slightly.

Preheat oven to 350 degrees. Spoon filling evenly into bread cups. Sprinkle cheese over tops. Bake 8 to 10 minutes or until cheese melts. Serve warm.
Yield: 36 croustades

These tiny tidbits are packed with flavor: *(clockwise from left)* Mushroom and Chicken Pastries are easy to make with purchased puff pastry dough. Carnitas are miniature tacos with a sausage filling. Mushroom Croustades offer a creamy combination of sausage and mushrooms in a toasted bread cup.

(Right) Take your party south of the border with quick-and-easy Chicken Fajitas. Marinate the chicken ahead of time in our special mixture of tequila and spices; then prepare these zesty morsels in minutes.

CHICKEN FAJITAS

½ cup vegetable oil
1 cup tequila
½ cup lime juice
¼ cup tomato paste
2 garlic cloves, minced
1 whole jalapeño pepper
½ teaspoon salt
½ teaspoon chili powder
½ teaspoon cumin
1½ pounds boneless, skinless chicken breast, cut into strips
10 flour tortillas for fajitas
3 tablespoons vegetable oil
1 large bell pepper, cut into strips
1 large onion, cut into strips

Guacamole, sour cream, salsa, and grated Cheddar cheese to serve

In a glass bowl or baking dish, combine ½ cup oil, tequila, lime juice, tomato paste, garlic, jalapeño, salt, chili powder, and cumin. Blend well. Add chicken, cover, and marinate in refrigerator at least 6 hours or overnight.

Preheat oven to 350 degrees. Wrap tortillas in aluminum foil. Bake 15 minutes while preparing fajitas.

Remove chicken from marinade. In a large, heavy skillet over medium-high heat, heat 3 tablespoons oil. Add chicken and cook, stirring constantly, 5 to 7 minutes or until chicken is done. Add bell pepper and onion and cook 2 to 3 minutes more, just until vegetables are crisp-tender. Serve with tortillas, guacamole, sour cream, salsa, and cheese.
Yield: 10 fajitas

For a change of pace, serve Middle Eastern Sesame Spread with Toasted Pita Chips. Top with coconut, chutney, almonds, or raisins.

SESAME SPREAD WITH TOASTED PITA CHIPS

  ⅓ cup tahini (roasted sesame paste)
  1 can (15 ounces) garbanzo beans, drained
  ⅓ cup lemon juice
  ¼ cup chopped green onion
  1 garlic clove, minced
  ¼ teaspoon salt
  ¼ teaspoon freshly ground pepper
  1 tablespoon minced fresh parsley
     Pita bread

     Coconut, chutney, toasted slivered almonds, and golden raisins to serve

Combine first eight ingredients in a blender or food processor and process until smooth. Pack mixture into a small bowl, cover and refrigerate at least 1 hour before serving.

Preheat oven to 450 degrees. Separate pita rounds in half. Cut each circle into 8 wedges. Place on ungreased baking sheet. Bake 5 to 8 minutes or until lightly browned and crisp. Serve sesame spread on pita chips. Top chips with coconut, chutney, almonds, and golden raisins.

Yield: about 1½ cups of spread

A zesty blend of crabmeat and shrimp, Hot Creole Seafood Dip will spice up your party.

HOT CREOLE SEAFOOD DIP

- 2 tablespoons butter or margarine
- ½ cup chopped bell pepper
- 1 green onion, chopped
- 1 package (8 ounces) cream cheese, softened
- 1 tablespoon Worcestershire sauce
- 3 to 4 drops hot pepper sauce
- 1½ teaspoons Creole seasoning
- ½ teaspoon chili powder
- ⅛ teaspoon cayenne pepper
- 2 cans (6½ ounces each) lump crabmeat, drained
- 1 package (5 ounces) small cooked shrimp

  Crackers to serve

In a small skillet, melt butter over medium-high heat. Add bell pepper and green onion and sauté 3 minutes; set aside.

In a large saucepan, melt cream cheese over low heat. Add pepper mixture, Worcestershire, hot pepper sauce, Creole seasoning, chili powder, and cayenne. Stir in crabmeat and shrimp, blending well. Cook until heated through. Serve warm with crackers. May be served in a chafing dish.
Yield: about 3½ cups of dip

LONDON BROIL

- 1½ teaspoons salt
- 1 teaspoon granulated sugar
- 2 tablespoons minced onion
- ½ teaspoon dry mustard
- ½ teaspoon Italian seasoning
- ¼ teaspoon ground ginger
- ½ teaspoon freshly ground pepper
- ¼ cup lemon juice
- ½ cup vegetable oil
- 1 garlic clove, minced
- 1 flank steak (about 2 pounds)

  Purchased hors d'oeuvre-size buns to serve
  Mustard and mayonnaise to serve

Combine all ingredients except steak, blending well. Place steak in a glass or enamel baking dish. Cover with marinade mixture and refrigerate at least 6 hours or overnight, turning steak occasionally.

Preheat broiler. Remove steak from marinade and broil about 5" from heat for 5 to 6 minutes on each side. Meat should be rare. Cut steak diagonally across the grain in thin slices. Serve with buns, mustard, and mayonnaise.
Yield: enough meat for about 36 buns

LAMB'S WOOL

- 3 apples, peeled and chopped
- 3 tablespoons butter or margarine
- 3 bottles (12 ounces each) dark beer
- ½ cup firmly packed brown sugar
- 1 teaspoon ground cinnamon
- 1 teaspoon ground ginger
- ½ teaspoon ground nutmeg

Preheat oven to 350 degrees. Place apples in baking dish; dot with butter. Bake 30 minutes.

In a large saucepan, combine apples, beer, brown sugar, and spices. Cook, stirring occasionally, over medium-low heat until heated through. Serve warm.
Yield: 6 to 8 servings

A hot spiced ale made with apples and dark beer, Lamb's Wool is a perfect accompaniment to London Broil, a marinated rare steak served on a bun with mayonnaise and spicy mustard.

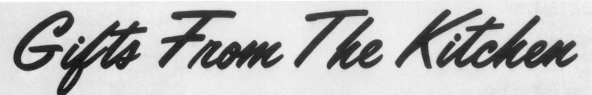

Gifts From The Kitchen

Home-cooked gifts created in your kitchen are truly gifts from the heart. As you lovingly prepare them, a little bit of yourself goes into each and every gift you make. And because each recipe is carefully chosen to fit that special someone's tastes, your homemade goodies reflect an extra touch of love. To help with your gift-giving, this section includes lots of ideas for delicious offerings, along with attractive ways to present them.

Any of these flavorful condiments makes a tasty gift: Garlic and Horseradish Jellies *(top basket)* are delicious with meats or cream cheese and crackers. Christmas Antipasto *(top left)*, Marinated Vegetables *(top right)*, and Candied Baby Dills *(bottom left)* make zesty additions to a relish tray. Our gourmet mustards — Garlic, Horseradish, Peppercorn, and Curried *(center and bottom baskets)* — are easily made from purchased mustards. Painted wooden hearts make great labels and gift tags.

CHRISTMAS ANTIPASTO

- ⅓ cup garlic wine vinegar
- 1 cup vegetable oil
- 1 cup olive oil
- 1 teaspoon salt
- ½ teaspoon freshly ground pepper
- 2 tablespoons lemon juice
- 1 teaspoon dry mustard
- 1 teaspoon paprika
- ¼ teaspoon cayenne pepper
- 1 teaspoon oregano leaves
- ½ teaspoon basil leaves
- ½ teaspoon green peppercorns
- 1 jar (7 ounces) roasted peppers, drained
- 2 cans (14 ounces each) artichoke hearts, drained

Combine the first 12 ingredients and blend well. Place remaining ingredients in a jar with a tight-fitting lid. Pour dressing over vegetables; shake to blend. Allow mixture to marinate overnight at room temperature.
Yield: about 3½ cups of antipasto

CANDIED BABY DILLS

- 1 quart miniature dill pickles
- 2 cups granulated sugar
- ½ cup apple cider vinegar
- 1 tablespoon fancy pickling spice
- ½ teaspoon garlic salt

Drain pickles in colander; rinse. Combine remaining ingredients in a large saucepan and bring to a boil. Remove from heat and cool. Pack pickles into sterilized jar(s) and pour syrup over pickles. Cap jar(s) and refrigerate overnight to allow flavors to blend.
Yield: 1 quart of pickles

MARINATED VEGETABLES

- ½ cup sherry wine vinegar
- 1½ cups vegetable oil
- ½ cup olive oil
- 1 teaspoon salt
- 1½ teaspoons dry mustard
- 1 teaspoon tarragon leaves
- ½ teaspoon lemon peel
- 1½ cups pickled okra, drained
- 1½ cups baby corn, drained
- 8 to 10 cherry peppers

For dressing, combine the first 7 ingredients and blend well. Place remaining ingredients in a jar with a tight-fitting lid. Pour dressing over vegetables; shake to blend. Allow mixture to marinate overnight at room temperature.
Yield: about 4½ cups of vegetables

GARLIC JELLY

- 2 tablespoons butter or margarine
- 1 head garlic, cloves separated, peeled, and minced
- 3 cups granulated sugar
- ½ cup apple cider vinegar
- 6 ounces liquid pectin

In a large saucepan, combine butter and garlic over medium heat. Cook, stirring constantly, until garlic is light golden brown (3 to 4 minutes). Add sugar and vinegar. Cook, stirring constantly, until sugar dissolves and mixture comes to a boil. Stir in pectin. Boil 1 minute, stirring constantly. Remove from heat. Skim foam from top of jelly. Pour into sterilized jars and seal.
Yield: about 3 cups of jelly

HORSERADISH JELLY

- 3 cups granulated sugar
- ½ cup prepared horseradish
- ½ cup apple cider vinegar
- 6 ounces liquid pectin

In a large saucepan, combine sugar, horseradish, and vinegar over medium heat. Cook, stirring constantly, until sugar dissolves and mixture comes to a boil. Stir in pectin. Boil 1 minute, stirring constantly. Remove from heat. Skim foam from top of jelly. Pour into sterilized jars and seal.
Yield: about 3 cups of jelly

GARLIC MUSTARD

- 8 garlic cloves, peeled
- 1 tablespoon olive oil
- 1 jar (8 ounces) Dijon-style mustard
- ½ teaspoon basil leaves
- ¼ teaspoon oregano leaves

Preheat oven to 325 degrees. Place garlic in a small baking dish and drizzle with oil. Roast garlic 20 to 30 minutes, stirring frequently, until garlic is soft. Mash garlic, removing any tough pieces.
Combine mashed garlic with remaining ingredients and refrigerate overnight to allow flavors to blend.
Yield: about 1 cup of mustard

HORSERADISH MUSTARD

- 1 jar (8 ounces) sweet, hot mustard
- 2 tablespoons prepared horseradish
- ¼ teaspoon garlic salt
- ¼ teaspoon ground allspice
- ¼ teaspoon cayenne pepper

Combine all ingredients and refrigerate overnight to allow flavors to blend.
Yield: about 1 cup of mustard

CURRIED BROWN MUSTARD

- 1 jar (8 ounces) spicy brown mustard
- 1½ teaspoons lemon pepper
- 1 teaspoon curry powder
- ½ teaspoon grated lemon peel

Combine all ingredients and refrigerate overnight to allow flavors to blend.
Yield: about 1 cup of mustard

PEPPERCORN MUSTARD

- 1 jar (8 ounces) country Dijon-style mustard
- 1 tablespoon crushed green peppercorns
- ½ teaspoon tarragon leaves
- ¼ teaspoon ground allspice
- ¼ teaspoon salt

Combine all ingredients and refrigerate overnight to allow flavors to blend.
Yield: about 1 cup of mustard

For someone who's nuts about peanuts, try these treats: *(clockwise from top left)* Kids will flip for Peanut Butter Spread served with graham cracker bears. Grown-ups will savor creamy Miniature Honey-Roasted Peanut Cheesecakes; we wrapped ours in cellophane and tied it with a bright ribbon. Peanut Butter-Cheese Shorties combine two favorite flavors. For unique gift tags, use a paint pen to label shiny glass ornaments.

PEANUT BUTTER SPREAD

- 1 jar (16 ounces) peanut butter
- 2 tablespoons honey
- 1 cup miniature semisweet chocolate chips
- ½ cup chopped miniature marshmallows
- ½ cup chopped salted peanuts

Combine all ingredients in a microwave-proof container, blending well. Microwave on high power 1 minute and gently stir to swirl mixture. (Do not overcook; chocolate will soften when stirred.) Spoon into gift container. Serve with graham crackers or vanilla wafers.
Yield: about 3 cups of spread

MINIATURE HONEY-ROASTED PEANUT CHEESECAKES

- 2 cups crushed chocolate-covered graham crackers
- 3 packages (8 ounces each) cream cheese, softened
- 1 cup peanut butter
- 1½ cups honey
- 2 teaspoons vanilla extract
- 1 cup whipping cream
- 4 eggs
- 1 cup chopped roasted peanuts
- 1 cup miniature semisweet chocolate chips

Preheat oven to 325 degrees. Line bottoms of four 5-inch springform pans with circles of aluminum foil. Lightly grease pans. Press ½ cup graham cracker crumbs into bottom of each pan; set aside.

In a large mixing bowl, beat cream cheese until smooth. Beat in peanut butter, honey, vanilla, and cream. Beat in eggs until well blended. Stir in peanuts and chocolate chips. Divide mixture evenly between the four pans. Bake 40 to 45 minutes or until centers are set. Cool to room temperature. Cover and refrigerate overnight. To remove springform, use a knife to loosen sides of cheesecake from pan; remove springform. Store in refrigerator.
Yield: 4 cheesecakes

PEANUT BUTTER-CHEESE SHORTIES

- ¼ cup butter or margarine, softened
- ¾ cup smooth peanut butter
- 1¼ cups all-purpose flour
- ½ teaspoon salt
- 8 ounces mild Cheddar cheese, grated
- ¼ cup water

Preheat oven to 400 degrees. In a large mixing bowl, combine all ingredients, blending well. On a lightly floured surface, use a floured rolling pin to roll out dough to ⅛-inch thickness. Using a pastry wheel or knife dipped in flour, cut dough in ½ x 2-inch strips. Transfer strips to lightly greased baking sheets. Bake 10 to 15 minutes or until golden brown. Cool before removing from pans. Store in airtight container.
Yield: about 9 dozen shorties

Tea lovers will enjoy curling up with a cup of hot spiced tea made with our Mulled Tea Bag. For a cute gift, include a basket of Santa Cinnamon Sticks to stir the tea.

MULLED TEA BAG

2½ teaspoons loose tea leaves
2 whole cloves
3 whole allspice berries
1 teaspoon coarsely crushed cinnamon stick
½ teaspoon grated orange rind
¼ teaspoon grated lemon rind
5-inch square of fine-mesh cheesecloth
Cotton string

Place tea leaves, cloves, allspice, cinnamon, and orange and lemon rind on cheesecloth square. Bring corners together and tie into a bag with string. To brew tea, place bag in a mug and add 6 ounces boiling water; steep 4 to 5 minutes.
Yield: 1 tea bag

SANTA CINNAMON STICKS

For each Santa stick, you will need one approx. 6" long cinnamon stick; red, flesh, black, and pink acrylic paint; small paintbrush; small, stiff paintbrush; and Duncan Snow Accents™ (available at craft stores).

Note: Refer to photo to paint Santa, allowing to dry between colors. Painted area of stick should not extend below rim of cup.

1. For hat, paint ½" of one end of stick red. For face, paint ¾" below hat flesh; paint eyes black and cheeks pink.
2. Use stiff brush and Snow Accents™ to paint beard, eyebrows, and hat trim.

147

These little cookies make very special gifts: Flavored with brown sugar and pecans, tiny Heart Cookies are packaged in a box bearing a heartfelt message. "Painted" with icing to resemble old-fashioned stoneware, pretty Pottery Tea Cakes can be presented in a miniature crock tied with a raffia bow.

POTTERY TEA CAKES

COOKIES
- 1 cup butter, softened
- 1 cup granulated sugar
- 1 egg
- 2 teaspoons vanilla extract
- 3 cups all-purpose flour
- 1 teaspoon baking powder
- ½ teaspoon salt
- ½ cup milk

ICING
- 2 cups confectioners sugar
- 1 egg white
- 2 teaspoons water
- Blue paste food coloring

In a large mixing bowl, cream butter, sugar, egg, and vanilla. In a separate bowl, combine flour, baking powder, and salt. Stir flour mixture into butter mixture alternating with milk. Wrap dough in plastic wrap and refrigerate overnight.

Preheat oven to 375 degrees. Trace pattern onto tracing paper and cut out. On a lightly floured surface, use a floured rolling pin to roll out dough to ⅛-inch thickness. Use a paring knife to cut around pattern or use cookie cutter to cut out dough. Transfer cookies to lightly greased baking sheets and bake 8 to 10 minutes or until cookies are lightly browned around the edges. Remove from pans and cool on wire racks.

In a small mixing bowl, combine confectioners sugar, egg white, and water. Divide icing in half and add blue food coloring to half of icing. Ice cookies with white icing; allow to dry. Referring to photo, use a pastry bag fitted with a small round tip and filled with blue icing to pipe designs. To make sponged cookies, use crumpled plastic wrap to stamp blue icing on cookies.

Yield: about 9 dozen tea cakes

HEART COOKIES

½ cup butter, softened
⅓ cup firmly packed brown sugar
1¼ cups all-purpose flour
½ cup ground toasted pecans
1 teaspoon vanilla extract

Combine all ingredients in a medium mixing bowl, blending well. Wrap dough in plastic wrap and refrigerate 1 hour.

Preheat oven to 350 degrees. On a lightly floured surface, use a floured rolling pin to roll out dough to ¼-inch thickness. Using a 1-inch wide heart-shaped cookie cutter, cut out dough. Transfer cookies to ungreased baking sheets. Bake 10 to 15 minutes or until golden brown. Remove from pans and cool on wire racks.
Yield: about 6 dozen cookies

HEART COOKIE BOX

You will need one sheet of natural parchment paper; 4" dia. round Shaker box; brown water-based stain; blue acrylic paint; foam brushes; matte Mod Podge® sealer; graphite transfer paper; Design Master® glossy wood tone spray (available at craft stores); a soft cloth; black permanent felt-tip calligraphy pen with fine point; tracing paper; small, sharp scissors; and matte clear acrylic spray.

1. Paint entire box and lid with blue paint; allow to dry. Apply stain to entire box and lid, wiping off excess with soft cloth; allow to dry.
2. Lightly spray one side (right side) of parchment paper with wood tone spray; allow to dry.
3. Trace heart-in-hand pattern onto tracing paper. Use transfer paper to transfer pattern to wrong side of parchment paper. Cut out design.
4. For paper strip on side of lid, measure the width and the circumference of side of lid. Cut a piece of parchment paper the determined measurements plus ½" in length (piece as necessary). Use pen to write "Here's my heart in my hand" in center of strip. Spray strip with three coats of acrylic spray, allowing to dry between coats.
5. Refer to photo and use Mod Podge® to glue wrong side of hand cutout and paper strip in place. Apply two coats of Mod Podge® to box and lid, allowing to dry between coats.

Cut in heart, moon, and star shapes, Santa Cookies decorated with colorful frosting and bits of licorice will delight young and old alike.

SANTA COOKIES

COOKIES

½ cup butter or margarine, softened
½ cup shortening
1 cup granulated sugar
1½ teaspoons vanilla extract
3 eggs
3½ cups all-purpose flour
2 teaspoons cream of tartar

ICING

3 cups confectioners sugar
¼ cup butter or margarine, softened
¼ cup milk
1 teaspoon vanilla extract
Red food coloring
Small pieces of black licorice for decoration

In a large mixing bowl, cream butter, shortening, sugar, and vanilla. Beat in eggs one at a time, beating well after each addition. Stir in flour and cream of tartar.

Wrap dough in plastic wrap and refrigerate at least 2 hours.

Preheat oven to 425 degrees. On a lightly floured surface, use a floured rolling pin to roll out dough to ⅛-inch thickness. Cut out dough using star, moon, or heart-shaped cookie cutters. Transfer cookies to lightly greased baking sheets and bake 6 to 8 minutes or until lightly browned around edges. Remove from pans and cool on wire racks.

Combine all icing ingredients except food coloring in a medium mixing bowl, blending until smooth. Divide icing in half and add red food coloring to half of icing. Referring to photo, ice cookies with red icing. Use a pastry bag fitted with a small round tip and filled with white icing to pipe beards and trim. Decorate with small pieces of licorice.
Yield: about 6 dozen cookies

Inspired by visions of Santa's sweetshop, we created this selection for all the good boys and girls on your list: Quick-and-easy Oriental Snack Mix *(top left)* blends crunchy pretzels and chow mein noodles with golden raisins, peanuts, and white chocolate. Decorated with "holly" made of candied cherries, White Chocolate Fudge *(top right)* is another delectable treat. Your friends will find it hard to believe that these Chocolate Billionaires *(center left)* are homemade! The adorable Santa-shaped Lollipops *(center right)* are easy to make with purchased candies. Colorful tissue paper makes festive wrappers for Honey Taffy *(in drawer)*, and Chocolate-Covered Cherries *(bottom left)* are wonderfully rich.

LOLLIPOPS

Crush pieces of same-colored clear, hard candies. Preheat oven to 300 degrees. Place lightly oiled metal lollipop molds on a baking sheet, propping molds level with crumpled aluminum foil. Fill molds with crushed candy. Bake 10 minutes or until candy melts. Remove from oven and insert lollipop sticks into candies. Allow candies to cool. Gently press backs of molds to release candies.

WHITE CHOCOLATE FUDGE

3 cups granulated sugar
¾ cup butter or margarine
⅔ cup half and half
12 ounces white chocolate
1 jar (7 ounces) marshmallow cream
1 cup coconut
1 cup chopped toasted almonds

Small pieces of candied red and green cherries for garnish

In a large, heavy saucepan, combine sugar, butter, and half and half. Bring to a boil over medium heat, stirring constantly. Continue stirring and boil 5 minutes. Remove from heat. Add chocolate and stir until melted. Stir in remaining ingredients. Pour into a greased 13 x 9 x 2-inch pan; cool. Cut into squares. If desired, decorate with pieces of red and green cherries to resemble holly.
Yield: about 45 pieces of fudge

CHOCOLATE-COVERED CHERRIES

3½ cups confectioners sugar
¼ cup butter or margarine, softened
3 tablespoons crème de cocoa liqueur
1 tablespoon milk
1 tablespoon vanilla extract
About 60 maraschino cherries with stems, drained and patted dry
12 ounces white or semisweet chocolate
⅓ bar paraffin

In a large mixing bowl, combine sugar, butter, crème de cocoa, milk, and vanilla; mix well. Mold a small amount of mixture around each cherry, being careful to completely enclose cherry with mixture. Place on waxed paper.

In top of a double boiler over warm water, melt desired chocolate with paraffin. Dip cherries in chocolate and return to waxed paper. Allow chocolate to set at room temperature. Check bottoms of cherries and reseal with additional melted chocolate if necessary. If desired, drizzle tops of candies with additional melted chocolate. Cover loosely and store in a cool place at least two days to form cordial (do not refrigerate). Store in airtight container.
Yield: about 60 candies

ORIENTAL SNACK MIX

2 cups small pretzels
1½ cups golden raisins
1 cup chow mein noodles
1 cup salted peanuts
18 ounces white chocolate
¼ bar paraffin

In a large mixing bowl, combine pretzels, raisins, chow mein noodles, and peanuts.

In top of a double boiler over warm water, combine chocolate and paraffin. Heat just to melting point, stirring constantly. Remove from heat and quickly stir into pretzel mixture. Spread mixture on a lightly greased baking sheet. Refrigerate 10 minutes or until set. Break candy into bite-size pieces. Store in airtight container.
Yield: about 2¾ pounds of candy

CHOCOLATE BILLIONAIRES

1 package (14 ounces) caramels
3 tablespoons water
1½ cups coarsely chopped pecans
1 cup coarsely crushed crisp rice cereal
2 cups milk chocolate chips
⅓ bar paraffin

In top of a double boiler over low heat, melt caramels with water. Remove from heat and stir in pecans and cereal. Drop by rounded teaspoonfuls onto lightly greased waxed paper. Chill until firm.

In top of a double boiler over low heat, melt chocolate chips and paraffin. Dip candies in chocolate; place on waxed paper and chill until set. Store in airtight container.
Yield: about 4 dozen candies

HONEY TAFFY

3 cups granulated sugar
1 cup whipping cream
1 cup honey
1 tablespoon butter or margarine
⅛ teaspoon salt

Combine all ingredients in a large, heavy saucepan. Bring to a boil over medium heat, stirring constantly. Continue stirring and cook until mixture reaches soft-crack stage (270 degrees on a candy thermometer). Pour mixture onto a cool, buttered surface. Allow mixture to cool slightly (enough so that it can be handled comfortably). Pull taffy into ropes (color will lighten slightly). Break ropes into pieces about 2 inches long. Wrap each piece of candy in waxed paper and twist ends. If desired, wrap red and green tissue over waxed paper.
Yield: about 2¾ pounds of candy

A pretty presentation makes a gift of food even more memorable. Scrumptious Cranberry Muffins tucked in a reusable holiday tin are perfect for breakfast or an afternoon snack. Nestled on a lacy paper doily and topped with a ribbon rose, rich Fudge Pound Cake is an elegant gift. To craft your own roses, see page 156.

CRANBERRY MUFFINS

MUFFINS
- 3 cups all-purpose flour
- ¾ cup granulated sugar
- 1 tablespoon baking powder
- ½ cup milk
- ½ cup butter or margarine, melted
- 2 eggs
- 1 tablespoon vanilla extract
- 1½ cups chopped fresh cranberries
- ¾ cup chopped pecans
- 1 tablespoon grated orange peel

TOPPING
- 1½ teaspoons grated orange peel
- ¼ cup granulated sugar
- 1 teaspoon ground cinnamon
- ¼ cup chopped pecans

Preheat oven to 375 degrees. For muffins, combine flour, sugar, and baking powder in a large mixing bowl. Make a well in center of mixture and add milk, butter, eggs, and vanilla. Stir just until all ingredients are moistened (batter will be lumpy). Stir in remaining ingredients. Fill greased or paper-lined muffin cups two-thirds full with batter.

In a small bowl, combine topping ingredients. Sprinkle topping over muffins. Bake 25 to 30 minutes or until a muffin springs back when gently pressed.

Yield: about 2 dozen muffins

FUDGE POUND CAKE

- ½ cup butter or margarine, softened
- 1¾ cups granulated sugar
- 2 teaspoons vanilla extract
- 3 eggs
- 1¾ cups all-purpose flour
- ⅔ cup cocoa
- 2 teaspoons baking powder
- ½ teaspoon baking soda
- 1 cup sour cream

Preheat oven to 325 degrees. In a large mixing bowl, cream butter, sugar, and vanilla. Beat in eggs.

In a separate bowl, combine flour, cocoa, baking powder, and baking soda. Blend flour mixture into butter mixture alternating with sour cream. Pour into a greased 9 x 5 x 3-inch loaf pan. Bake 1 hour and 20 minutes or until a toothpick inserted in center comes out clean. Cool 10 minutes in pan; remove from pan and cool completely.

Yield: one cake

Jolly Good Snacks

Your friends will love these tastes from the British Isles: Named for that lovable character created by Charles Dickens, Oliver Twists *(left)* are perfect for dunking in a hot drink; you may even want to tuck a tin of special tea in your gift basket, too. The Irish Cream Cakes, loaded with chocolate chips and rich liqueur flavor, are so wonderful that everyone will want you to give them year after year — and you won't mind when you see how easy they are to make! Baking these little treats in miniature shapes adds a festive touch.

OLIVER TWISTS

    1 package (4 ounces) crystallized
         ginger
    ½ cup butter or margarine, softened
    ¼ cup honey
    1 cup granulated sugar
    2 eggs
    3¼ cups all-purpose flour
    1½ teaspoons baking powder
    ½ teaspoon salt
         Granulated sugar

In a blender or food processor, process ginger until very fine; set aside.

In a large mixing bowl, cream butter, honey, and sugar until light and fluffy. Beat in eggs until smooth. Blend in ginger.

In a separate bowl, combine flour, baking powder, and salt. Stir flour mixture into creamed mixture. Wrap dough in plastic wrap and refrigerate overnight.

Preheat oven to 325 degrees. Roll small amounts of dough into ¼ x 10-inch ropes; form into pretzel shapes. Transfer cookies to lightly greased baking sheets and sprinkle with sugar. Bake 20 to 25 minutes or until lightly browned. (Cookies will be slightly firm to touch and will become crisper as they cool.) Remove cookies from pans and cool on wire racks. Store in airtight container.
Yield: about 3 dozen cookies

IRISH CREAM CAKES

CAKES

    1 package (18.5 ounces) white cake
         mix
    1 package (6 ounces) instant vanilla
         pudding mix
    1½ cups Irish Cream liqueur
    1 cup miniature semisweet
         chocolate chips
    4 eggs
    ½ cup vegetable oil

GLAZE

    1 cup Irish Cream liqueur
    3 cups confectioners sugar

Preheat oven to 350 degrees. In a large mixing bowl, combine all cake ingredients and blend well. Pour into 10 greased and floured 1-cup metal gelatin or cake molds. Bake 25 to 30 minutes or until cake springs back when lightly touched.

In a small bowl, combine glaze ingredients, blending well. While cakes are still warm in pans, poke holes in cakes; pour liqueur mixture over. Allow cakes to cool in pans at least 2 hours before removing from pans.
Yield: 10 miniature cakes

Festive Santa Bread

Sweet Santa Bread is sure to delight both children and grown-ups! And because every loaf rises differently while baking, each Santa will have his own distinct personality.

SANTA BREAD

BREAD

    2   packages active dry yeast
   4½   cups all-purpose flour, divided
    ½   cup granulated sugar
    2   teaspoons grated orange peel
    2   teaspoons ground cinnamon
    1   teaspoon salt
    1   cup milk
    ¼   cup water
    ½   cup butter or margarine, softened
    2   eggs
    1   egg white
    1   tablespoon water
         Red paste food coloring
         Raisins and candied cherry halves

ICING

   2½   cups confectioners sugar
    3 to 4 tablespoons hot water
    ½   teaspoon vanilla extract

In a large mixing bowl, combine yeast, 1¼ cups flour, sugar, orange peel, cinnamon, and salt; set aside.

In a saucepan, heat milk, ¼ cup water, and butter just until butter melts. Add mixture to dry ingredients, beating until smooth. Beat in eggs and 1¼ cups additional flour. By hand, stir in enough of remaining flour to make a stiff dough. Turn onto a floured surface and knead until smooth and elastic, about 8 to 10 minutes. Place dough in a greased bowl, turning once to grease top. Cover and let rise 1 hour, or until doubled in bulk.

Preheat oven to 350 degrees. Punch down dough; divide in half and refer to photo to form two Santa heads. Place on greased baking sheet.

In a small bowl, combine egg white, tablespoon water, and food coloring. Use pastry brush to paint hats. Bake 40 to 45 minutes or until bread sounds hollow when tapped. Remove from pan and cool on wire rack.

Blend icing ingredients. Ice beards. For eyes and noses, attach raisins and cherries with dots of icing.
Yield: 2 loaves of bread

Lads and lassies will love these adorable Anise Shortbread Scotties! Cut in the shape of this popular dog and adorned with an iced holly "collar," the light, crispy cookies are flavored with just a hint of licorice. For a true Highland treat, present them in a handsome Tartan Shaker Box, patterned after the Tartanware that was so popular during Queen Victoria's reign in the 1800's.

ANISE SHORTBREAD SCOTTIES

    1   cup butter, softened
    ½   cup confectioners sugar
    1   teaspoon vanilla extract
  1½   teaspoons crushed anise seed
    ¼   teaspoon ground cinnamon
    2   cups all-purpose flour
        Granulated sugar

Cream butter and confectioners sugar, beating until light and fluffy. Beat in vanilla, anise seed, and cinnamon. Stir in flour.

Trace pattern onto tracing paper and cut out. On a lightly floured surface, use a floured rolling pin to roll out dough to ¼-inch thickness. Use pattern and paring knife to cut out cookies. Transfer cookies to ungreased baking sheets. Sprinkle with granulated sugar. Chill cookies 30 minutes before baking.

Preheat oven to 375 degrees. Bake cookies 5 minutes, reduce heat to 300 degrees, and bake 10 minutes more. Remove from pans and cool on wire racks.

Yield: about 4 dozen cookies

TARTAN SHAKER BOXES

For each box, you will need desired size Shaker box, tartan fabric, grosgrain ribbon the width of side of lid, craft glue, desired color acrylic paint, and paintbrush.

1. Paint inside of box and lid; allow to dry.
2. To cover lid, cut fabric ½" larger than box lid. Center lid on wrong side of fabric circle and glue edges of fabric to side of lid. Glue ribbon to side of lid, covering raw edges of fabric.
3. To cover box, determine length of fabric by measuring the circumference of box and adding ½". Determine width of fabric by measuring the height of box and adding ½". Cut fabric determined measurements. With one long edge even with top of box, glue fabric to side of box, overlapping short edges. Glue remaining long edge to bottom of box.

TRANSFERRING PATTERNS

When entire pattern is shown, place a piece of tracing paper over pattern and trace pattern, marking all placement symbols and openings. Cut out traced pattern.

When one-half of pattern is shown, fold tracing paper in half and place folded edge along dashed line of pattern. Trace pattern, marking all placement symbols and openings. Cut out traced pattern; open pattern and lay it flat.

SEWING SHAPES

1. Center pattern on wrong side of one piece of fabric and use a fabric marking pencil to draw around pattern. If indicated on pattern, mark opening for turning. **DO NOT CUT OUT SHAPE.**

2. With right sides facing and leaving an opening for turning, carefully sew fabric pieces together **directly on pencil line.**

3. Leaving a ¼" seam allowance, cut out shape. Clip seam allowance at curves and corners. Turn shape right side out. Use the rounded end of a small crochet hook to completely turn small areas.

4. If pattern has facial features or detail lines, use fabric marking pencil to lightly mark placement of features or lines.

BLOCKING STITCHED PIECES

1. To remove transfer lines from a stitched piece, wash piece in cool water with mild white soap. Rinse thoroughly in cool water. Gently squeeze out excess water. **DO NOT WRING.**

2. Lay stitched piece flat on a clean, white towel. Roll piece in towel to absorb excess moisture.

3. To block stitched piece, place piece on blocking board and align fabric threads with vertical and horizontal lines on board. Pulling fabric taut so that all wrinkles are removed, use T-pins, spaced ¼" apart, to pin stitched piece to board. Allow to dry. Remove pins.

RIBBON ROSES

For each rose, you will need 18" of 2¼"w grosgrain ribbon, a velvet leaf, 18-gauge florist wire, and green crepe florist tape.

1. Following **Fig. 1**, place ribbon on a flat surface and fold left end at a 45 degree angle, leaving a 1" tail.

Fig. 1

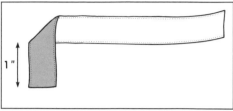

2. To form center of rose, roll left edge of ribbon to inside (**Fig. 2**).

Fig. 2

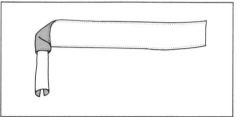

3. To form petals, twist top edge of ribbon back as shown in **Fig. 3**. Again roll left edge to inside until left edge is near the end of the twist. At this point, twist top edge of ribbon to back again (**Fig. 4**). Continue rolling and twisting until end of ribbon is 1" long.

Fig. 3

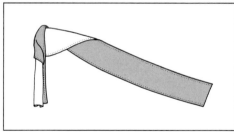

Fig. 4

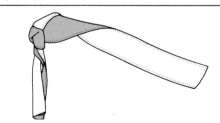

4. Holding ends of ribbon together, wrap one end of a 9" piece of florist wire around bottom of rose. Twist tightly to secure ribbon. Excess wire will be used for stem. Trim ribbon ends to ½". Place velvet leaf under rose. Wrap ribbon ends, leaf stem, and wire with florist tape.

CROSS STITCH

COUNTED CROSS STITCH

Work one Cross Stitch to correspond to each colored square on the chart. For horizontal rows, work stitches in two journeys (**Fig. 1**). For vertical rows, complete each stitch as shown in **Fig. 2**. When working over two fabric threads, work Cross Stitch as shown in **Fig. 3**. When the chart shows a Backstitch crossing a colored square (**Fig. 4**), a Cross Stitch (**Fig. 1, 2,** or **3**) should be worked first; then the Backstitch (**Fig. 7**) should be worked on top of the Cross Stitch.

Fig. 1

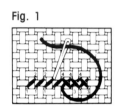

Fig. 2   **Fig. 3**

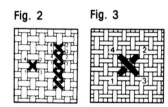

Fig. 4

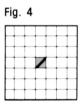

QUARTER STITCH (¼X)

Quarter Stitches are denoted by triangular shapes of color on the chart and on the color key. When working over two fabric threads, come up at 1 and go down at 2 as shown in **Fig. 5**.

Fig. 5

HALF CROSS STITCH (½X)

This stitch is one journey of the Cross Stitch and is worked from lower left to upper right. **Fig. 6** shows the Half Cross Stitch when working over 2 fabric threads.

Fig. 6

BACKSTITCH

For outline detail, Backstitch (shown on chart and on color key by black or colored straight lines) should be worked after the design has been completed (**Fig. 7**).

Fig. 7

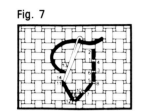

NEEDLEPOINT

GOBELIN STITCH

The Gobelin Stitch can be worked vertically, diagonally, or horizontally (**Fig. 1**). The number of threads each stitch is worked over may vary according to the chart.

Fig. 1

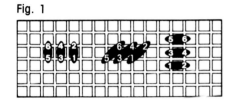

CROCHET

HALF DOUBLE CROCHET

To begin a half double crochet, wind yarn once over hook, bringing yarn from back over top of hook. Insert hook into ridge of chain or under V of stitch. Hook yarn and draw through. There should now be three loops on hook (**Fig. 1**). Hook yarn and draw through all three loops. One half double crochet is now complete.

Fig. 1

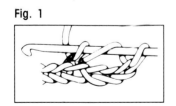

DOUBLE CROCHET

To begin a double crochet, wind yarn once over hook, bringing yarn from back over top of hook. Insert hook into ridge of chain or under V of stitch. Hook yarn and draw through. There should now be three loops on hook (**Fig. 2**). Hook yarn again and draw through the first two loops on hook (**Fig. 3**). Two loops should remain on hook. Hook yarn again and draw through remaining two loops (**Fig. 4**). One double crochet is now complete.

Fig. 2

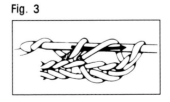

Fig. 3

Fig. 4

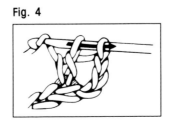

KNITTING

KNITTING

Hold the needle with the stitches in your left hand and the empty needle in your right hand. With the yarn in back of the needles, insert the right needle into the front of the stitch closest to the tip of the left needle from left to right. Bring the yarn beneath the right needle and between the needles from back to front (**Fig. 1**). Bring the right needle, with the loop of yarn, toward you and through the stitch (**Fig. 2**); slip the old stitch off the left needle.

Fig. 1

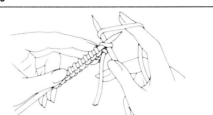

Fig. 2

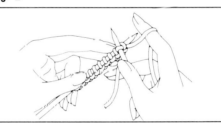

PURLING

Hold the needle with the stitches in your left hand and the empty needle in your right hand. With the yarn in front of the needles, insert the right needle into the front of the stitch closest to the tip of the left needle from right to left. Bring the yarn between the needles from right to left and around the right needle (**Fig. 3**). Move the right needle, with the loop of yarn, through the stitch and away from you (**Fig. 4**); slip the old stitch off the left needle.

Fig. 3

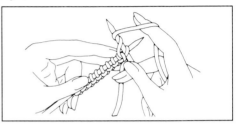

Fig. 4

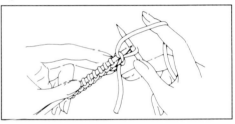

TREBLE CROCHET

To begin a treble crochet, wind yarn twice over hook, bringing yarn from back over top of hook. Insert hook into ridge of chain or under V of stitch. Hook yarn and draw through. There should now be four loops on hook. Hook yarn again (**Fig. 5**) and draw through the first two loops on hook. Three loops should remain on hook. Hook yarn again and draw through two more loops. Two loops should remain on hook. Hook yarn once more and draw through remaining two loops. One treble crochet is now complete.

Fig. 5

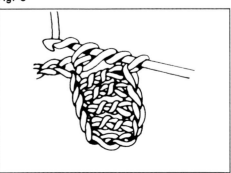

Continued on page 158

EMBROIDERY STITCH DIAGRAMS

FRENCH KNOT

Bring needle up at 1. Wrap thread once around needle and insert needle at 2, holding end of thread with non-stitching fingers (**Fig. 1**). Tighten knot; then pull needle through fabric, holding thread until it must be released. For a larger knot, use more strands; wrap only once.

Fig. 1

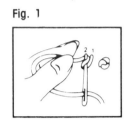

COLONIAL KNOT

This is a variation of a French Knot. Bring thread up at 1, and wrap around needle. Bring thread over needle and back under (**Fig. 2**) to form a figure eight. Insert needle close to 1, holding end of thread with non-stitching fingers. Tighten knot; then pull needle through fabric, holding thread until it must be released.

Fig. 2

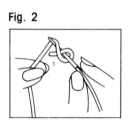

STRAIGHT STITCH

Come up at 1 and go down at 2 (**Fig. 3**).

Fig. 3

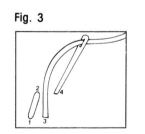

RUNNING STITCH

Make a series of straight stitches with stitch length equal to the space between stitches (**Fig. 4**).

Fig. 4

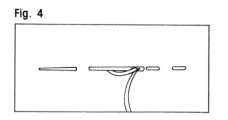

OUTLINE STITCH

Following **Fig. 5**, come up at 1. Keeping the thread above the stitching line, go down at 2 and come up at 3. Go down at 4 and come up at 5.

Fig. 5

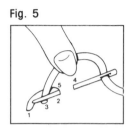

STEM STITCH

Following **Fig. 6**, come up at 1. Keeping the thread below the stitching line, go down at 2 and come up at 3. Go down at 4 and come up at 5.

Fig. 6

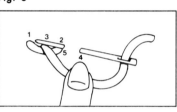

COUCHED STITCH

Come up at 1 and go down at 2, following line to be couched. Work tiny stitches over floss to secure (**Fig. 7**).

Fig. 7

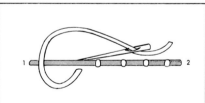

LAZY DAISY STITCH

Following **Fig. 8**, come up at 1 and make a counterclockwise loop with the thread. Go down at 1 and come up at 2, keeping the thread below the point of the needle. Secure loop by bringing thread over loop and going down at 2.

Fig. 8

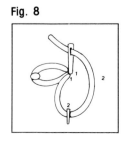

BUTTONHOLE STITCH

Bring needle up at 1; go down at 2 and back up at 3 with needle on top of floss (**Fig. 9a**). Work stitches close together but not overlapping (**Fig. 9b**).

Fig. 9a

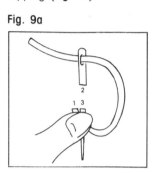

Fig. 9b

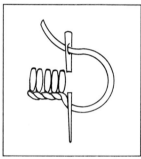

SATIN STITCH

Following **Fig. 10**, come up at odd numbers and go down at even numbers with the stitches touching but not overlapping.

Fig. 10

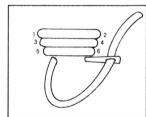

PADDED SATIN STITCH

Work a pad layer of Satin Stitch in direction **opposite** that of Satin Stitch which will be on top. (**Note:** Arrows on chart indicate direction to stitch each layer.) Following **Fig. 11**, work second layer of Satin Stitch over pad layer.

Fig. 11

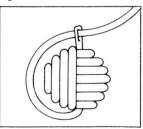

CREDITS

We want to extend a warm thank you to the generous people who allowed us to photograph our projects in their homes.

- *Winter Wonderland*: Gordon and Kelly Holt
- *A Christmas Homecoming*: Joan Gould
- *Southwest Celebration*: Dr. Lynnah Selman
- *Romancing Christmas*: Jimmy and Dot Woodruff
- *Country Holiday*: Nancy Newell

We especially thank the Department of Arkansas Heritage for allowing us to photograph *A Wee Merry Christmas* in the Arkansas Territorial Restoration. We also thank Pulaski Academy for allowing us to photograph our *Yearbook Shirt* on their campus.

To Marty Mack of Stained Glass Overlay, Little Rock, Arkansas, we send our warmest appreciation for his enthusiasm and skillful craftsmanship in creating the beautiful window on our front cover.

We're grateful to the businesses and private individuals who contributed some of the accessories shown in our photographs.

- Kathy Hagins: Green and white quilt, pages 9 and 11, and red and white quilt, page 20
- Lynne Haubenreich: Willow furniture, pages 9 and 11
- Westmoore Pottery of Seagrove, North Carolina: Pottery, pages 112, 113, 114, 115, and 117

To Magna IV Engravers of Little Rock, Arkansas, we say thank you for the superb color reproduction and excellent pre-press preparation.

We want to especially thank photographers Ken West, Larry Pennington, and Mark Mathews of Peerless Photography, Little Rock, Arkansas, for their time, patience, and excellent work.

To the talented designers who helped in the creation of many of the projects in this book, we extend a special word of thanks.

- *Animal Angels*, page 80: Sandy Belt
- *Christmas Sweatshirt*, page 105: Polly Carbonari
- *Joyful Christmas*, page 67: Needlework adaptation by Kathy Rose Bradley
- *Mantel Scarf*, page 14, and *Snowbird Stocking*, page 15: Diane Brakefield

We extend a sincere thank you to all the people who assisted in making and testing the projects in this book: Jean Black, Jennie Black, Janet Boyeskie, Margaret Bredlow, Deborah Burns, Martha Jean Cobb, Debra Dove, Anita Drennan, Trudi Drinkwater, Dianna Ferguson, Lynnette Haugen, Johnnie Mac Henry, Helen Hood, Catherine Hubmann, Phyllis Lundy, Marcia Phillips, Carol Reed, Tracy Rhein, Georganne Ricks, Patti Sowers, Laurie Terpstra, Karen Tyler, and Janet Yearby. And a special word of thanks is given for the busy hands of Catherine Spann and Pat Johnson.

Enjoy HOLIDAY TOUCHES
in your home
for 21 days FREE

If you love country …
If you love holidays …
You'll love this treasury of
heartwarming decorations

There's nothing more inviting than a country home — especially when it's decorated for the holidays. Inside our new book, *Holiday Touches for the Country Home*, you'll find dozens of homespun projects — including lots of quick-and-easy ones — to blend with your country decor. The holidays and special occasions featured are Valentine's Day, St. Patrick's Day, Easter, Mother's and Father's Days, patriotic days, Halloween, Thanksgiving, and Christmas. This exciting 128-page treasury is the second book in our Memories in the Making series, which began with *Gifts of Good Taste*.

**ALSO AVAILABLE
AT NEEDLECRAFT SHOPS**

CALL TOLL-FREE 1-800-423-1780

(In Florida, 1-800-858-0095)

To review *Holiday Touches* free in your home for 21 days, call the toll-free number on this page or write to Leisure Arts, *Holiday Touches*, P.O. Box 420047, Palm Coast, FL 32142-0047. If you like our book, pay just $18.95 (in U.S. funds) plus postage and handling. If not completely delighted, you may return the book within 21 days and owe nothing.

If you keep it, we will automatically send you, **on approval**, future books in the Memories in the Making series. You are in no way obligated to buy any future books, and you may cancel at any time just by notifying us. Please allow 6-8 weeks for delivery. Limited time offer.